Women, Men, and the Bible

Women, Men, and the Bible

Revised Edition
with Study Guide

Virginia Ramey Mollenkott

1989

The Crossroad Publishing Company
370 Lexington Avenue, New York, N.Y. 10017

Printed in the United States of America

Library of Congress Cataloging-in-Publication Data

Mollenkott, Virginia R.
  Women, men, and the Bible/Virginia Ramey Mollenkott.—Rev. ed.
  p. cm.
  ISBN 0-8245-0893-9 (pbk.):
  1. Woman (Christian theology) 2. Woman (Theology)—Biblical
teaching. I. Title.
BT704.M64 1988   88-20422
261.8'344—dc19   CIP

Contents

v

112382

Introduction to the Revised Edition

Since 1976 when I wrote the first version of *Women, Men, and the Bible*, the Christian feminist movement has become considerably more sophisticated, finely tuned, and mature. Resources abound concerning inclusive language, gender stereotyping, equal partnership marriage, female ordination and ministry, the metaphorical nature of theology, feminist interpretation of the Bible, and other topics touched upon in this book. Why, then, a revised edition?

It seems to me that *Women, Men, and the Bible* is still one of the very few books that consider adult interpersonal politics in the light of the Bible approached as a unified and coherent reading experience. My doctorate is in literature, and I have spent three and a half decades teaching college young people how to read with greater attention to the details of the text. I approach the canonical Hebrew and Christian Scriptures as a single unit that may be expected to make sense and yield important insights if and when it is read with decent attention to historical, grammatical, and literary context. I approach the Bible not only wholistically but also with the hermeneutical norms and methods of the Christian feminist—a person committed *not* to female supremacy, but to human mutuality and equal partnership out of respect for God's image in us all.

Many resources now exist that are more specialized, more narrowly focused, and more detailed within their chosen parameters. *Women, Men, and the Bible* is simply an easy-to-comprehend introduction to some of the most basic concerns of Christian feminism.

During the past decade, the Religious Right has mounted a deadly backlash against the emancipation of women. As a consequence, people may be looking for a preliminary overview to clear away some of the misconceptions and fears that have been generated about human liberation, about women, about men, and about the Bible.

I have welcomed the opportunity to revise this book because I have experienced some valuable growth since 1976. Perhaps my greatest transformation has come through my membership in Women of Faith in the 80's, an inter-religious task force that meets either at the American Jewish Committee or National Council of Churches headquarters. (For further information, interested readers might turn to *Women of Faith in Dialogue*, a book I edited in 1987.) After seven years of interacting with Jewish, Muslim, Roman Catholic, and mainline Protestant women, I experienced tremendous shock at rereading some of my own wording in the earlier edition of *Women, Men, and the Bible.* In 1976, I had no intention of implying that the Jews had invented patriarchy. I knew that all of recorded history is the story of patriarchal civilization; that Jesus the feminist had lived and died as a Jew and would have been astonished to hear himself called "Christian"; that many of his early followers were Jews; that the Old Testament I revered so highly was shared with Christians by Jewish courtesy; that most of the New Testament was written by Jews, and interlaced with Jewish wisdom; and that Judaism is an ongoing, valid, and major world religion. I thought it would be obvious to everybody that my primary target was *Christian* patriarchalism.

But after years of glimpsing the world from various angles shared with me by my Jewish sisters and friends, some of my previous wording seemed to me absolutely appalling. Although financial pressures have made a massive rewriting impossible—apart from the introduction and study guide, I had to stay within the original word limit—I have attempted to renuance my argument. The errors that remain are my responsibility, since I was able to change only what I could no longer tolerate. But any improvement is due to inter-religious dialogue and the work of feminist theologians like Elisabeth Schüssler Fiorenza, Judith Plaskow, and Carter Heyward.

Some of my later books have developed in greater depth ideas that I touched upon in this one. I mention them for the sake of readers who might like to follow up on one or several ideas. The irrational fear that feminism might lead to the homosexualization of society (very briefly mentioned here) should be laid to rest by *Is the Homosexual My Neighbor? Another Christian View*, which I wrote with Letha Scanzoni in 1978. Chapter Three of *Women, Men, and the Bible* was expanded by *The Divine Feminine: Biblical Imagery of God as Female* (1983) and by *An Inclusive Lectionary: Readings for Years A,B, and C*, prepared by a National Council of Churches committee on which I had the privilege of serving. I further developed a concept (only incipient here) of all people of faith as a corporately "Christed" New Humanity in *Godding: The Bible and Human Responsibility* (1987).

Women, Men, and the Bible targets patriarchalism as a Christian heresy and hence necessarily interprets the whole Bible from a Christian perspective. I have therefore retained much of the Christian terminology of the earlier version. But I have attempted to be more humanly inclusive in the nuancing of that terminology.

Whenever I have quoted from a specific version of the Bible, I have placed any inclusive language changes in square brackets so that they will be immediately evident to the reader.

Despite being questioned through the years by people who find the word *submission* unsavory or offensive, even when modified by the word *mutual*, I have decided to stick to the term *mutual submission*. Submission connotes self-sacrifice; and indeed the normal compromises and adjustments required by any life-partnership often do entail a certain amount of suffering. "Submitting yourselves to one another out of reverence for Christ" seems to me to involve giving up some autonomy in order to gain the pleasures of attachment and community. Submission is in fact the price-tag of community; but health and justice demand that submission must be *mutual*, not unilateral.

Finally, I have supplied a study guide that can be used either by individuals or by groups meeting for perhaps six discussion sessions. I would suggest that individuals who are interested in self-discovery, or those who plan to lead group discussions, answer the study questions for each chapter *before* reading the relevant chapter.

Virginia Ramey Mollenkott

1
The Christian Way of Relating

Books are pouring off the presses concerning women's liberation, the role and status of women in the modern world, and
the proper relationship between Christian men and women in
the home and in the church. Almost every conceivable kind of
advice has been given. At the traditional extreme, Youth
Conflicts Seminar leader Bill Gothard teaches a chain of command in which the husband is God's hammer and the wife is
the chisel; by the action of the hammer on the chisel, the
children (the diamonds in the rough) are shaped. The military
phrasing of *chain of command* and the passivity of the chisel as
opposed to the activity of the hammer make clear the wife's
subordinate role in the home. Meanwhile, *Fascinating
Womanhood* advises that by cultivating cute, childish charms,
women can manipulate men into giving them anything they
want. *The Total Woman* adds sexy seductiveness to childish
charm but still advocates that Christian women be submissive
to their men and get what they want through coy manipulation. On the other hand, *All We're Meant to Be* teaches that an
honest and equal partnership is the most successful form of
male-female relating. And at the opposite extreme, *The First
Sex* advocates female supremacy. Where is truth in all this?
How is a person to know what is right and what is wrong?

It is my assumption that if we are interested in understanding the Christian way of relating to others, the Bible must be
our central source, and the teachings and behavior of Jesus
must provide our major standard of judgment. Jesus said very

little about relationships between women and men, and, as far as we know, he did not marry. But he did teach some important basic principles about how human beings ought to relate to one another. And he was very clear about the qualities which make a person truly great, authoritative, and important in the eyes of God. By studying Jesus' principles and observing his behavior against the background of first-century society, we can achieve a clear concept of the Christian way of relating.

At the historical moment when Jesus was born into the world, the status of women everywhere was very low. Although the Hebrew Scriptures reveal some cultic practices which are distressing to modern women, such as the need for ritual cleansing after menstruation and childbirth (with twice as much cleansing needed after girl babies than after boy babies), there is rarely any *contempt* for women taught in its pages.[1] By the time of Jesus' birth, however, many decades of commentary and custom had surrounded the canonical literature. And some of these traditions had considerably lowered the status of women. Males were taught to thank God daily that they were male (the prayer is recorded in the Talmud, Menachoth 43b).[2] Boy babies were regarded as a sign of God's favor as opposed to girl babies. Men avoided speaking to women in public, even their own women, because the tradition taught that a woman's voice was a sexual enticement (Berachoth 24a in the Talmud). Women were not permitted to read from the Torah during prayer services because of "the dignity of the congregation" (Megillah 23a). Women were not even permitted to pray aloud at their own table; the Berachoth 20b went so far as to pronounce a curse on any man who allowed his wife to recite the blessing over wine on behalf of the whole family. Some even considered it preferable to burn the Torah rather than to place it into female hands. The Talmud records Rabbi Eliezer's opinion that "whoever teaches his daughter Torah teaches her lasciviousness" (Sotah 3:4). In

Alexandria during the time of Jesus, the philosopher Philo Judaeus equated the masculine with reason and the feminine with sensuality—and, of course, taught males to condemn sensuality and to seek the reasonable life. In fact, Philo flatly stated that sexual desire was the "beginning of iniquities and transgressions." Had there been no Eve, Adam would have remained happy and immortal. Of course, such views could find plenty of support in Greek thought, especially in Aristotle's division of humanity into the Greek males as "headpersons," or dominators, and the females, slaves, and non-Greeks as "body-persons," or persons meant by nature to be dominated.

Divorce was easily accessible to men. The school of Hillel (Gamaliel's grandfather) taught that a man could divorce his wife if she spoiled his cooking, while Rabbi Akiba said that a man could divorce his wife if he found a woman more beautiful that she (Gittin 9:10). These views won out over the view of the school of Shammai that adultery was the only cause for divorce; so the position of the average woman was perilous indeed. A woman who appeared in public without a head covering or spoke to men in the street or even spoke too loudly at home was not entitled to a financial settlement at the time of divorce.

The apocryphal book of Ecclesiasticus, written about 180 years before Christ and preserved in Greek and Latin but recently discovered in a Hebrew text among the Dead Sea Scrolls, gives us a glimpse of the kind of scorn sometimes heaped upon women: "For out of clothes comes the moth, / and out of woman comes woman's wickedness. / Better a man's wickedness than a woman's goodness; / it is woman who brings shame and disgrace" (Ecclesiasticus 42:13–14 NEB). The Shabbath, a tractate in the Talmud which dates from the time of Jesus, flatly states that woman is "light-minded" (unreliable) and describes woman as being" a pitcher full of filth with its mouth full of blood" (Shabbath 152a). Although these were

probably minority opinions and although many first-century
Jewish wives were no doubt deeply loved, nevertheless it is
indicative of low *official* regard for women that such statements could be retained in literature valued as holy. As one
rabbinical dictum put it, "The world cannot exist without
males and females, but happy is he whose children are sons
and woe to him whose children are daughters."

Only through marriage and motherhood could a woman
hope to find respect or dignified status. She was not even a
complete person until marriage, for the Talmud declares, "A
woman is shapeless lump *[golem]*, and concludes a covenant
[of marriage] only with him who transforms her (into) a
(useful) vessel, as it is written [Isaiah 54:5]: *For thy maker is
thy husband*" (Babylonian Talmud, Sanhedrin 22*b*).

Against such a background we can begin to understand the
reason, when Jesus' disciples returned from grocery shopping
and found the Master talking with a Samaritan woman, they
were amazed (John 4:27). They had too much respect for Jesus
to question his wisdom outright ("Why are you talking to a
woman?"). But John admits that they would have liked to ask
him that very question. How their amazement must have
grown when they discovered that not only was he speaking to
a woman in the open—where he might be observed by other
men—but he was discussing advanced theology with her! And
despite the fact that she was a Samaritan—many people
looked down on Samaritans—and despite the fact that she was
living in sin, Jesus commissioned her as his special messenger
to her own city. John tells us that "many of the Samaritans
from that town believed in him because of the woman's testi-
mony" (John 4:39 NIV).

The more we find out about the cultural conditions of Jesus'
day, the more we realize that in situations like the con-
versation with the Samaritan woman, Jesus was deliberately
breaking customs which were degrading to the self-concept of

women. He was providing object lessons for his disciples—and for us all.

Other revealing incidents include the time Jesus was touched by a woman who had been hemorrhaging for twelve years. This woman had been ritually unclean all the time and would have rendered unclean any man whom she touched. No wonder she chose to touch the hem of Jesus' robe secretly! She hoped to get her healing without making a scene and without forcing him to undergo ritual cleansing. (She was probably acting on the principle that what he didn't know wouldn't hurt him.) When he called attention to her by asking who had touched him, her heart must have sunk—thinking that she was going to get bawled out for her nerve and lack of consideration. After all, *he* was a rabbi conducting important business, and *she* was just a "nobody" who had rendered him unclean! But instead of bawling her out he complimented her on her healing faith: " 'Take heart, daughter,' he said, 'your faith has healed you' " (Matthew 9:22 NIV).

It seems especially significant that Jesus took pains to locate the healing within the poor despised woman's faith rather than in himself or in the male establishment or even in God the Father. "*Your faith* has healed you"! Surely he was healing her inner feelings about herself as well as her superficial issue of blood. And he did not wash his clothes, bathe in water, and segregate himself until evening (Leviticus 15:27). Neither did he instruct the woman to segregate herself for seven days and then to make expiation by sacrificing two pigeons at the temple (Leviticus 15:28–30). He simply proceeded on his errand of raising the ruler's daughter from the dead.

Symbolically as well as literally, Jesus spent that memorable day raising women from the dead. By the object lesson of his own behavior, he showed that the ancient blood taboos no longer should operate to make women unclean half of their lives; he restored a woman's self-respect; and he again violated the taboo against speaking to women in public.

Early one morning, John tells us, some religious leaders brought to Jesus a woman taken in the very act of adultery (John 8:4). They referred Jesus to the law of Moses which said that the penalty of adultery was stoning, in order to see whether he would support or defy the law. If he defied the law, they would have strong evidence to harm him; if he upheld the law, they would still have the pleasure of asserting their own righteousness by stoning the poor, guilty woman to death. The interesting thing here is that if the woman was taken in the very act, certainly there was a man with her at the moment of discovery. And the law of Moses plainly stated that "both the adulterer and the adulteress shall be put to death" (Leviticus 20:10*b* RSV).

It is indicative of the despised condition of women in the first-century that the male accusers had released the adulterer and brought only the adulteress to be stoned to death. Even in the modern world, laws against prostitutes are often fully enforced, while their customers are almost never punished! But as we all know, Jesus refused to support a double standard of morality. He asked that only the *sinless* males should stone the woman. The oldest and most respected men in the crowd were the first to recognize Jesus' meaning and to slink away in embarrassment.

Finally, even the youngest and most self-righteous men were gone, and only the trembling woman was left with Jesus. He asked her, "Woman, where are they? Has no one condemned you?" She answered, "No one, sir." His response must have sounded incredibly beautiful to her ears: "Then neither do I condemn you. . . . Go now and leave your life of sin" (John 8:10–11 NIV).

If the sexual behavior of this woman was a sign of low self-respect and of desperate attempts to win male approval, it is doubtful that she would ever again have *needed* to commit adultery. Jesus had shown her that she was acceptable. Far from being less than the men who had condemned her, she was as good as they. In fact, she was far better off than they, because the only sinless man in the crowd, Jesus himself, had refused to condemn her.

Similarly, when religious leaders tried to trap Jesus into supporting their double standard of divorce by which a man could easily divorce his wife while the woman had no recourse whatsoever, Jesus flatly refused to do so. They asked him, "Is it lawful for a man to divorce his wife for any and every reason?" (Matthew 19:3 NIV). But Jesus referred to the creation narrative, to the creation of male and female as one flesh, in order to smash the double standard and to reassert God's ideal of human unity. And he insisted that the same rules which apply to women apply also to men: "I tell you that anyone who divorces his wife, except for marital unfaithfulness, . . . and . . . marries [another] woman . . . commits adultery" (Matthew 5:32 NIV).

In the first century as in the twentieth century, it was natural for people to locate evil somewhere outside of themselves. Rapists frequently try to blame their lust on their victims: "Why did she wear a blouse like that if she didn't want to be raped? She was asking for it." Leaving aside the intricacies of individual situations since women, like men, are by no means sinless, it is important to notice that Jesus had no time for such rationalizations. During the Sermon on the Mount, he commented, "You have heard that it was said, 'Do not commit adultery.' But I tell you that anyone who looks at a woman lustfully has already committed adultery with her in his heart" (Matthew 5:27–28). This is obviously not a condemnation of sexual desire within marriage, because within marriage sexual intercourse would not be adulterous. It is a condemnation of regarding other people as sexual objects and mentally undressing those with whom the observer has no commitment and therefore no privileges. Jesus was condemning any sexual fantasizing which uses other people as objects.

Instead of pandering to the tendency to blame others for one's own lust, Jesus comments that mental wallowing in irresponsible sexuality is sin. Immediately thereafter, in Matthew 5:31–32, he asserts the single standard of divorce which he repeats in Matthew 19—another indication that the real point of all this is the single standard of morality for both men and women. Ultimately, he is asserting responsible *personhood*. To most first-century people, men were persons and women were property to be used or disposed of at the pleasure of men. But to Jesus, women were persons just as fully as men.

Proof of Jesus' concern for full female personhood arises when a well-meaning woman shouts praise for Christ by focusing exclusively on the biological functions of his mother: "Happy the womb that carried you and the breasts that suckled you!" (Luke 11:27 NEB). By this language, Mary is reduced to one womb and two breasts. It is understandable that a first-century woman should think of herself in these terms since she had been socialized to think of herself and other women only as wives and mothers, almost exclusively as biological creatures. But Jesus will have none of it. He immediately redefines blessedness in a way which transcends either male or female biology: "Rather, blessed are they that hear the word of God, and keep it" (Luke 11:28). Certainly his purpose is not to deny that his mother is blessed. But he says she is blessed because she responded positively to the word of God, not simply because she became a mother—even his mother.

By Jesus' definition, for women as well as for men, biology is not destiny. Rather, spiritual commitment is destiny. According to Jesus, true blessedness is open to single women or childless women as well as to mothers, and to men and children as well as to women. Although Mary's particular role in divine and human history happened to involve her physical ability to bear a child, her blessedness stemmed not from her biological function, but from her internal willingness to cooperate with the larger plan of God. The same kind of blessedness is available to every person, Jesus implies, whether that person happens to be male or female, able or disabled, old or young, single or married. His response is unusual for any era but especially for an era in which women were valued chiefly as wives, mothers, and facilitators of male careers.

Jesus also affirmed the right of female persons to study the theology which had traditionally been closed to them. When Martha complained that Mary was not helping her with the housework but rather was studying the word of God at the feet of Jesus, the rabbi refused to order Mary to play the stereotypical female role. Instead, he praised Mary's sense of priorities: "'Martha, Martha,' the [Sovereign] answered, 'you are worried and upset about many things, but only one thing is needed. Mary has chosen what is better, and it will not be taken away from her'" (Luke 10:41–42 NIV). I do not consider this a put-down of those who must perform necessary household chores. Rather, Jesus is correcting Martha for allowing the multitude of mundane details to obscure for her the central value of spiritual growth. All of us, male and female, must struggle against the tendency to let life's details distract us from eternal values.

Jesus praised Mary for being single-minded enough to see and take advantage of the most important opportunity at that moment in her life, the opportunity to learn the word of God. Had Martha also sat down at the feet of Jesus, it is entirely possible that when the proper moment came, he would have served the food himself, as he did on another occasion for the five thousand who had been listening to his teachings.

For modern men and women, an important factor in this story is that Jesus flouted the sexual stereotypes of his day, stereotypes which demanded that women must serve rather than learn the word of God. Jesus accepted Mary's desire to learn just as fully as he accepted the male disciples' desire. And remembering the customs of his culture, we can recognize how radically shocking to his contemporaries was the fact that Jesus traveled with female as well as male disciples. Luke 8:1–3 tells us that as Jesus "traveled about from one city and village to another" (NIV), he was accompanied not only by the twelve, but also by *many* women!

After his resurrection, Jesus very deliberately withheld the honor of his first resurrection appearance from John and Peter, who had been at the tomb on Easter morning, in order to reveal himself to Mary Magdalene. John 20:17 tells us that Jesus delivered to Mary Magdalene the message of his resurrection and its full significance: "Do not hold on to me, for I have not yet returned to the Father [and Mother]. Go instead to my brothers and tell them, 'I am returning . . . to my God and your God'" (NIV). In Jesus' societal context, women were not acceptable as witnesses in a court of law. By those standards, such an important message should have been entrusted only to men. But Jesus very deliberately reserved for Mary the vision of resurrected being and very deliberately entrusted the magnificent resurrection message to her. Once again, Jesus was creating an object lesson for the disciples concerning the full personhood and ministry of women. It is disheartening that after twenty centuries, many Christian churches still reject female ministry, and many Christian men and women still fail to treat women with the full human respect Jesus never failed to show.

On many occasions during his earthly ministry, Jesus spoke specifically of how his followers were supposed to relate to one another. Very often, his statements were made in response to squabbles among the male disciples concerning who among them was the greatest. Repeatedly, Jesus defined greatness in terms of humility and servanthood. For instance, when the disciples asked who was the greatest in the realm of heaven

(Matthew 18:1), Jesus called a little child into the middle of the group and commented that "whoever humbles [themselves] like this child is the greatest in the kingdom of heaven. And whoever welcomes a little child like this in my name welcomes me" (Matthew 18:4–5 NIV). This was, of course, a deliberate reversal of all the values in the world in which Jesus and his disciples were living. And it remains a complete reversal of worldly values here in the twentieth century. The fact is that very few people have ever believed or acted upon Jesus' definition of greatness.

Even Jesus' own disciples failed to grasp his repeated teaching that the Christian way of relating is mutual submission and mutual service. This is proved by the fact that at the Last Supper, just before Jesus went out to the Garden of Gethsemane to face his trial and anguish, the disciples were so out of touch with his spirit that once again they got into an argument over which of them should be considered the greatest. How painful it must have been for Jesus to be confronted with such selfishness at the hour of his own greatest need! For the umpteenth time he explained to them, "In the world, [rulers] lord it over their country's Benefactors. Not so with you: on the contrary, the highest among you must bear [themselves] like the youngest, the chief of you like a servant" (Luke 22:25–26 NEB). Jesus further clarified his point by continuing, "For who is greater—the one who sits at table or the servant who waits on [the table]? Surely the one who sits at table. Yet here am I among you like a servant."

In this passage Jesus several times contrasts ordinary ways of relating with transformed ways of relating. "In the world, [rulers] lord it over their subjects"; in other words, dominance and submission is the world's way of relating. The great people of the world system manifest their greatness by controlling the less great. Yet "here am I"—the ruler of the Jews, the Ruler of glory—"here am I among you like a servant."

For his second example Jesus contrasts those who serve the

meal with those who sit at the table to be served. Clearly, by any worldly standards, those who sit and are served are more important than those who stand and serve. But once again Jesus overturns worldly values by identifying himself as a servant. Here as elsewhere, Jesus was trying to teach his disciples (and all of us) that "whoever wants to become great among you must be your servant, and whoever wants to be first must be your slave—just as the [Human One] did not come to be served, but to serve (Matthew 20:26–28 NIV).

Like Jesus, the apostle Paul also teaches repeatedly that the Christian way of relating is the way of mutual service and mutual submission. For instance, in Galatians 5:13 Paul writes, "You, my [sisters and] brothers, were called to be free. But do not use your freedom to indulge your sinful nature; rather, serve one another in love" (NIV). And he continues, "The entire law is summed up in a single command: 'Love your neighbor as yourself.'" Certainly Paul recognizes that it is impossible to love and accept others if we do not love and accept ourselves. But his emphasis is on the Christian way of relating to other people, which is to think of others as *equally* important and *equally* as lovable as we seem to ourselves. "*Serve one another* in love."

Similarly, in Romans 12:10, Christians are reminded to "be devoted to one another in [sisterly and] brotherly love. Honor one another above yourselves" (NIV). And in Ephesians 4:2 we are told that we are to relate to one another by being "completely humble and gentle"; we are to "be patient, bearing with one another in love" (NIV). Clearly, the Christian way of relating to one another is by mutual submission and mutual service.

In case anybody should think that passages about Christian submission refer only to males' submitting to other males, Paul urges the Corinthians to "submit" to all the workers in the household of Stephanus "and to everyone who joins in the work and labors at it" (I Corinthians 16:16 NIV). Not only may we assume that there were women in the household of Stephanus, but we also have the explicit mention of Priscilla as one of those workers to whom the Christians are supposed to submit. Clearly Paul's criterion here is devotion to God's work, regardless of the gender of the worker. Devoted work should earn the recognition, respect, and submission of other Christians, Paul implies, regardless of sex-role stereotypes.

It is in the context of mutual submission that we must read the famous passages about the submission of Christian wives to their husbands, in particular Ephesians 5:22 and following. Here wives are told to *submit* to their husbands, and husbands are told to *love* their wives. Many Christians have made a big distinction between submitting and loving, but the distinction is not supported either by the teachings of Jesus or by the context in Ephesians 5. Immediately before saying "Wives, submit yourselves to your husbands as to the Lord," the text says that *all* of us should submit to one another "out of reverence for Christ." In fact, in the Greek, the verb for *submit* in verse 21 is carried over as understood in verse 22 so that a literal translation reads, "Being subject to one another in the fear of Christ, the wives to their own husbands as to the Lord." Since the verb for *wifely* submission (v. 22) is left out in dependence upon the verb for *mutual* submission (v. 21), there is absolutely no excuse for separating these two concepts.

Therefore, when Ephesians speaks of wives' submitting themselves to their husbands, it is building upon the concept that every Christian is intended to submit to every other Christian, to serve every other Christian, to defer lovingly to every other Christian. Women are to be subject to their husbands in everything, just as the whole church is subject to the Christ in everything; and because of reverence to God, because of subjection to God, every person is to be submissively concerned about the welfare of every other person.

The author makes very clear that the love which husbands are to show their wives is a love which involves the husband's submission. He establishes that principle by saying that husbands are to love their wives "just as Christ loved the church and gave self up for her" (Ephesians 5:25). The model for the husband to follow, therefore, is the self-emptying which Paul described in Philippians 2:3–8. Here again, just as in Ephesians 5, the text describes the Christian way of relating:

> Do nothing out of selfish ambition or vain conceit,
> but in humility consider others better than yourselves.
> . . . Your attitude should be the same as that of Christ
>   Jesus:
>   Who, being in very nature God,
>   did not consider equality with God something to be
>   grasped,
>   but made [of self] nothing,
>   taking the very
>   nature of a servant,
>   being made in human likeness.
> And being found in appearance [human]
>   humbled [the self]
>   and became obedient to death—even death on a
>   cross! (NIV)

The husband who loves his wife as Christ loved the church and gave self up for it is, therefore, just as submissive toward his wife as she is toward him, since each of them in honor prefers or defers to the other. The Christlike husband takes upon himself the form of a servant, humbles himself, and dies to himself by living for the best interests of his family. He loves his wife as he loves his own body, because he and his wife are one flesh.

In Colossians 3:18–19 Paul again tells Christian wives to submit to their husbands and Christian husbands to love their wives. Here again the context is significant. Immediately prior there are instructions that *all* Christians should be humble of mind, meek, patient, forgiving, loving and full of

gratitude to God (vv. 12–17). Immediately following the instructions about social relationships there is the reminder that
everybody is equal in the eyes of God (v. 29).

Through many centuries and even in our own time, there
are many Christians who read these and other passages as
teaching submission on the part of the wife and dominance on
the part of the husband. The only thing which is proved by
such readings is how totally we have forgotten both Christ's
and Paul's teachings concerning the Christian way of relating,
which is *mutual* submission and *mutual* service.

Similarly, many Christians read Peter's remarks concerning
wifely submission without paying any attention to the context,
which once again concerns the Christian way of relating.
I Peter 2:18–25 counsels servants to be subject to their masters "because Christ suffered for you, leaving you an example,
that you should follow in [those] steps." From there Peter
moves into a discussion of wifely submission, obedience, and
subjection (3:1–6) and then into instructions to husbands to
"in the same way be considerate as you live with your wives
and treat them with respect as the weaker partner and as heirs
with you of the gracious gift of life, so that nothing will hinder
your prayers" (3:7 NIV; emphasis mine). From there, Peter
moves into the widest sense of Christian community: "Finally,
all of you, live in harmony with one another; be sympathetic,
love as [sisters and] brothers, be compassionate and humble"
(3:8 NIV).

In other words, Peter is agreeing with Paul that *every*
Christian is supposed to demonstrate the spirit of Christ,
being full of compassion and courtesy and submissive love.
Husbands, wives, unmarried men, unmarried women—*all* of
us in the Christian community are intended to serve one
another and to defer to one another.

Peter says that the husband is to treat his wife with respect
for two reasons: because she is the weaker partner and because she is spiritually equal to him as the heir of the gift of

life. Modern experience does not bear out the concept that women are intellectually or physically weaker than men, since women live longer than men and after similar conditioning can often equal the physical and intellectual accomplishments of men. But Peter may have been referring to the common assumption of his own culture that women were both intellectually and physically weaker than men. Peter cannot be blamed for holding an assumption which, despite much evidence to the contrary, is still cherished by many people in the twentieth century!

On the other hand, it is quite probable that Peter was merely referring to the undisputed fact that first-century women were financially dependent upon men and therefore were the weaker partners in the marriage. We owe Peter a debt of enormous gratitude for pointing out that this economic weakness of women, this economic advantage of men, was not to be the cause of prideful male dominance but rather was to cause men to give women special respect. And Peter warns that if Christian men failed to give their wives the respect due to those who were weaker in worldly ways but equal in spiritual ways, their prayers would be hindered. In other words, Peter is saying that a man's relationship to God is conditional upon his relationship to his wife. Failure to respect her will damage his own spirit.

In I Peter 3 as in Ephesians 5, the basic topic is the Christian way of relating. Wives are to be subject to their husbands and husbands are to love and respect their wives, a loving and respecting which throughout the Christian scriptures involves willing submission and service. Just as we do not believe that wifely subjection excludes the wife from loving her husband, we should not believe that husbandly loving excludes the husband from subjection to his wife. The Christian way of relating is *mutual* submission and *mutual* service and *mutual* love.

How would mutual submission work out in a modern marriage? First, there would be no assumption that either partner is always right or is more important spiritually and hence should have the last word. There would be a careful assessment of gifts: whoever is better at finances might take charge of bill-paying, whoever cooks better might do most of the cooking, and so forth. In case of a radical difference of opinion about an important issue, such as whether the family should move to another city, the partners would work out the differences the way friends have worked out such differences for centuries: by discussing pros and cons, by trying to discern which partner's interests are most deeply concerned. The partner to whom the move makes *less* difference would logically be the one to defer in such a case in honor of the partner who cares terribly much. Perhaps there could be an agreement that the next major sacrifice would be made by the partner who had not deferred in this case. The important principle is that each person is viewed as equally vital and valid in the process of determining God's will for the family. And because of the equal validity, each seeks to serve the other out of love.

Frequently, mutual submission might mean that the more assertive and articulate partner would actually *teach* the less assertive partner how to argue more effectively and how to make his or her points more clearly. And surely one aspect of "in honor preferring one another" would be concern for each partner's self-concept. For instance, if a husband perceives that his wife has a very low view of her own worth, he might try to find ways to encourage her appreciation of her own personality and gifts. And because our society places such high value on *paid* work, he might calculate how much it would cost him to replace her services as homemaker, nurse, baby-sitter, and so forth. Either by actually paying her the amount she earns at the going rates for those services or by repeatedly expressing in detail his appreciation for them, he might help her to recognize her value in this area. Conversely, a wife might bolster her husband's self-image by frequently reiterating that his human worth is not to be measured by his annual income but rather by his values and relationships and simply his *being*. Thus each partner can help to heal the harm which society has done to the other partner.

An important question remains concerning the New Testament's treatment of marriage: Why do both Peter and Paul use terminology of obedience and submission concerning the wife's relationship to her husband and terminology of love and respect concerning the husband's relationship to his wife? Couldn't the apostles have headed off a lot of confusion by writing, instead, "Wives, be subject to your husbands, and husbands be subject to your wives"?

Certainly that message would have been much clearer here in the twentieth century. But we must remind ourselves of the background of Judaism and Greek and Roman religions into which the gospel was first introduced. Although we have concentrated our attention mainly on Judaism, because Jesus was a Jew, historian Sarah B. Pomeroy has made clear that the status of women in classical antiquity was similarly low in most practical respects. (Her findings are interestingly recorded in *Goddesses, Whores, Wives, and Slaves*, published in 1975 by Schocken Books.) As we have seen, some Jewish males tended to ignore even their own wives and daughters in public; yet Peter and Paul were telling them to love their wives as the Christ had loved them, to give themselves up for their wives as Jesus had given life up for them. What a revolutionary message! For the first-century apostles, the major mission was to spread the gospel. There were many things about the culture which were antichristian, including slavery and the male domination of women. But first things first. Although the New Testament would contain the principles which, when obeyed, would do away with slavery, racism, and male supremacy, it was important not to detract from the basic message of Jesus as Savior by trying to correct all social injustices overnight.

First-century Judaism, like classical Greek society, was extremely patriarchal. Men exercised great authority over their wives and children. It was radical enough for Jesus, Paul, and Peter to introduce the concept of women as spiritual equals, as complete human persons, meant to be loved as the Christ had loved the church. To have used overt terminology of husbandly submission to the wife would have totally alienated people who were conditioned to male supremacy. They would have been so shocked that they would have rejected everything else in the gospel message. (For that matter, many modern Christians seem to react in the same way!) It is apparently that sort of shock to which the author of Titus refers in chapter 2, verse 5, when he counsels that newly converted Christian wives should be subject to their husbands "so that no one will malign the word of God." He also counsels that newly converted slaves should be obedient to their masters "so that in every way they will make the teaching about God our Savior attractive" (2:10*b* NIV). Apparently the idea was not to discredit the gospel message by suddenly overthrowing all social custom.

Modern Jewish scholar Abraham Cohen thinks that the reason the first- and second-century rabbis were so opposed to giving women religious training was their fear that Jewish women would follow the example of many Christian women who were embracing celibacy. This view lends support to my contention that Peter and Paul were trying to avoid distracting people from the gospel message by too sudden a reaction against established customs. In spite of all their careful safeguards, however, some distraction did occur.

Instead of risking a sudden and perhaps catastrophic challenge to the whole social order, both Peter and Paul placed the expected remarks about wifely submission into a context of husbandly love and honor and dealt with the whole husband-wife relationship within a context of mutual submission, mutual compassion, and mutual loving service as the Christian way of relating. Certainly it is our fault if we fail to get their message, with the advantage of the whole New Testament and after all these centuries!

In order to get closer to the full initial impact of the New Testament on male-female relationships, let's try to imagine ourselves as first-century male converts to Christianity. We are taught that as new Christians we form the Body of Christ. We are the church. Naturally, we look upon our wives as inferior to ourselves both intellectually and physically, and it is no surprise to us when Peter and Paul tell our wives that they ought to be submissive and obedient to us. After all, even the unconverted wives are obedient to their husbands— that's the way things have always been, that's the way things are supposed to be!

But we are absolutely amazed to read that, according to Peter, we must *respect* our wives because they are "heirs [with us] of the gracious gift of life." In our culture it is the *men* who inherit things. We had never thought of our wives as the heirs to anything, let alone to the gracious gift of eternal life!

And we are even more stunned when we read that the apostle Paul compares our wives to the church. We ourselves are the church. But we are now told to love our wives as Jesus loved the church (that's us!) and gave up self for it (that is, for us!). Does that mean we can no longer assume we should always get our own way?

Jesus gave self up for us. We must give ourselves up for our wives. Our wives are identified with the church, which is us. We are one flesh. The whole relationship between us and our wives must change! We had thought that because we had held the purse strings, we had the right to lord it over our wives. But now we must change from the worldly way of relating, which assumes that the stronger can dominate the weaker, to the Christian way of relating, which assumes that everyone serves everyone else and especially that the stronger must *serve* the weaker!

And that brings us back to the question with which we began: Between men and women, should there be equality or should one submit to the other? The Bill Gothards and Marabel Morgans of modern evangelicalism are teaching that the biblical answer is the submission of the woman to the man. A few militants are pushing for the submission of the man to the woman or for sexual segregation. The vast majority of feminists are pleading for the equal-partnership of men and women. But the biblical answer is submission: not the submission of one category of persons to another category, but rather the voluntary and loving submission of each individual to all the others.

What happens when one partner obeys Christ by being submissive and concerned and the other partner sees the submission and concern only as an opportunity to exploit, dominate, and abuse? Of course, no one person can dictate to another how to handle such a sad and cruel situation, and the subject is a complex one. But the abused man or woman should certainly be aware that the abusing partner is in violation of the Scripture, which gives to neither male nor female the right to make a slave of another person. It is not the will of God for any human relationship to be full of hostility and attempts to humiliate and degrade. It is not the will of God for one person to refuse to help while the other person becomes exhausted with serving. Yet a good relationship cannot be achieved by one person alone, since by definition *relationship* involves at least two persons. Faced by an uncooperative and unbiblical partner, the abused individual must make the difficult decision of whether to suffer in hope of future improvement or to abandon the relationship in search of a more affirming life.[3]

Returning to our major thesis, it is vital to remember that

Christian equality is never a matter of jockeying for the dominant position. Christian equality is the result of mutual compassion, mutual concern, and mutual and voluntary loving service. The Christian way of relating achieves male-female equality through mutual submission.

2
The Patriarchal Way of Relating

As we have seen, the New Testament teaches that the Christian way of relating is through mutual submission and mutual and voluntary loving service. But as somebody once quipped: "Who ever said that Christianity hasn't worked? It's never even been *tried* yet!" Certainly the history of male-female relations through the centuries demonstrates that Jesus' teachings concerning mutual submission have at best received only lip service, and at worst have been converted into a cruel parody of themselves. Christlike submission has been taught to wives but not to husbands. Instead of giving themselves up for their wives as Jesus gave self up for the church, husbands have been encouraged to assume that their wives are supposed to make all the sacrifices.

This is hardly the place for a history of the oppression of women through the centuries. That sad story is told in such books as *The Subordinate Sex: A History of Attitudes Toward Women,* and *The First Sex.*[1] But the Christian reader of such books should be prepared to confront some angry and often unfair attacks on the Bible. The authors see the Bible as a repressive book, unconcerned with human justice, because that is the way it has been used by organized religion through the years.

There can be no serious question that Christianity as an organized religion has in many ways departed from the teachings of its own Scriptures. And nowhere has it departed more radically than by building up tremendous power structures.

Overtly in Roman Catholicism there is an enormous hierarchy in which the basic relational pattern is the patriarchal pattern of dominance and submission rather than the Christlike pattern of voluntary mutual service. But many Protestant churches have also lent their support to patriarchal dominance and repressive authoritarianism. The more I study the history of the churches as opposed to the actual teachings of Scripture, the weaker grow my objections to an angry accusation made by novelist Leo Tolstoy in 1893: "The Christian churches and Christianity have nothing in common save in name: they are utterly hostile opposites. The churches are arrogance, violence, usurpation, rigidity, death; Christianity is humility, penitence, submissiveness, progress, life."

What this means is that we must constantly guard against taking our interpretations of the Bible at second hand. Even at first hand we must diligently study to be sure we are understanding the spirit of the Book as it speaks to us and our contemporaries. In order to come to an accurate understanding of scriptural meaning, it is important for us to study the cultural background out of which sprang the various books of the Bible and to learn as much as we can from the generations of Bible scholars who have gone before us. Although, of course, one lifetime is too short to learn all we should know about the Bible, it is vital that we approach this most difficult and significant of books with humility and with all the background study we can muster. As theologian Bernard Ramm says, "Although the claim to by-pass mere human books and go right to the Bible itself sounds devout and spiritual, *it is a veiled egotism.*"[2]

Nowhere are the dangers of interpreting the Bible without adequate scholarship and careful concern for context more evident than in the dozens of books recently being published concerning male-female relationships in Christian churches and homes. Such books have become really big business, so that secular publishers are snatching at Christian titles. For instance, during the first year after Revell published Marabel Morgan's book *The Total Woman*, it sold 370,000 hardbound copies. Pocket Books bought the paperback rights for a cool $750,000, so that the book became available in almost any supermarket or drug store across the country. That would be cause for great rejoicing if *The Total Woman* portrayed a Christian way of relating. Unfortunately, what it portrays is the patriarchal power-game of dominance and submission carried into the most intimate of human relationships. The woman is told that for her own happiness, not only must she accept Jesus as Savior, but she must totally subordinate herself to her husband's pleasure. She must never resist his decision. She must wear various costumes and flimsy negligees to give him variety. She must call him at the office to tell him she craves his body. She must play dumb and weak to give him a sense of power. And she is told that all this is the will of God as revealed in the Bible. Courses in Total Womanhood are taught in hundreds of Christian churches all over America!

Marriage is not the only form of relating between Christian men and women; there are also male-female relationships within the church and the professional and business worlds. But because the family remains a central concern for the church and society and because attitudes concerning family structure set the tone for other male-female relationships, it is worth our while to concentrate on the kind of marital advice which has recently been offered to Christian husbands and wives under the guise of God's revealed will for the human race.

If my analysis of the Christian way of relating has been accurate—and I urge you to study the New Testament and to check every reference and context for yourself—and if what Christ and the apostles teach really is *mutual* submissive love and concern, then we may expect to find that human experience shows that this is indeed the healthiest, most adult, most positive form of marital relating. If, on the other hand, the

Bible really does teach that Christian wives must submit to their husbands with the husbands responsible before God to rule over the family unit, we may expect to find that marriages based on dominance and submission are healthier, more mature, and more positive than marriages based on mutual submission.

In *Men, Women, and Change,* an excellent sociological study of marriage and the family, Letha and John Scanzoni point out that there are four types of marital power-structure: the owner-property type, in which the husband has absolute power and the wife has none; the head-complement type, in which the husband has the vast majority of power and the wife has just a little; the senior-junior partnership type, in which the husband has most of the power but the wife shares a significant percentage of it; and the equal-partnership marriage, in which the power is fluid and is shared equally. The Scanzonis point out that the owner-property type of marriage was almost universal until this century, explaining that "a person's power over another person depends on the resources he or she holds out to that person, how dependent that second person is on these resources, and whether or not that second person can find alternate sources for the benefits elsewhere."[3] Therefore, it is because women now have the option of entering the work force that most modern marriages have shifted from the owner-property type to either the head-complement model or the senior partner-junior partner model, with the wives assuming more responsibility but still subordinating their careers to their husbands'. Very recently, however, there has been a move toward increasing numbers of equal-partnership marriages (p. 251).

Of course, marriage is a very individual matter, and, after all is said and done, a successful marriage can only be defined as one which satisfies and fulfills both partners. The remarkable thing about the Christian way of relating is that it can shed light and beauty within any one of these four marriage models. When society's economic structure conferred absolute power on the male, as it did until this century, fortunate indeed was the family in which the male was a true follower of Christ who sought to die to his own will. Such a husband and father responded to his family's dependency with self-giving love. Unfortunately, history reveals that such marriages were rare indeed and that absolute family power tended to corrupt absolutely.

Here in the twentieth century most Christian men and women are operating either under the head-complement or senior-junior partner marital structures, and, of course, either of them can produce genuine Christian marriages if both partners are fully and deeply concerned about serving the best interests of the other person. But a serious problem has arisen because many evangelical and fundamentalist Christian leaders have taken the position that equal-partnership marriages are contrary to the Bible. These leaders are trying to convince young people that all attempts in the equal-partnership direction are doomed to failure because they violate the revealed will of God. We have seen, however, that the Christian way of relating is a way of mutual submission and mutual service. There is no reason this Christian way of relating cannot work in an equal-partnership marriage. As a matter of fact, the equal-partnership marriage, with its sharing of child-related and household tasks and its equal concern for the careers of both husband and wife, provides a perfect opportunity for the practice of mutual submission and mutual loving service.

Perhaps the most disturbing feature of the many attacks on equal-partnership marriage is the assumption that the success of the marriage is almost entirely the responsibility of the wife. To discover that the success or failure of any marriage depends upon the efforts of both partners, not simply one of them, we need go no further than the *Ladies Home Journal* which runs a monthly column about marital difficulties entitled "Can This Marriage Be Saved?" Inevitably the counseling described in the column involves new insights and new adjustments for both the wife and the husband.

Dr. O. Quentin Hyder, formerly a medical missionary and now a practicing Christian psychiatrist, points out that in his experience "marriage problems are impossible to help unless both partners desire improvement in their marital relationship and are willing to come regularly. If motivation for treatment is unilateral [that is, of serious concern to only one member], the marriage is usually doomed."[4] According to this no-doubt-accurate observation, any self-help book about marriage would have to be addressed to both members of the relationship and would require concerned effort on the part of both. Yet most conservative Christian books lay the burden of marital success squarely on the shoulders of the woman, requiring all the psychological adjustments of her and blaming only her if success is not achieved.

In the process the husband is often lifted to the level of an absolute norm, as if he were God, while the wife is reduced to the worst kind of self-sacrificing idolatry. Self-sacrifice is beautiful when it is done as Christ did it: in absolute freedom as an expression of the deepest drives of the personality and without any interest in recompense. But the self-sacrifice now being urged upon the Christian wife is entirely different. It is not a choice freely made but rather a course of action so deeply ingrained by socialization and so connected with divine approval that the woman actually *has* no choice. When she begins to feel resentment about her own lack of fulfillment, unconsciously she begins to retaliate against her husband by "just happening" to burn his dinner or "just happening" to be perpetually too tired for sexual intercourse. And self-sacrifice for the children in the unconscious hope that they will in turn center their adult lives on their mother leads to either smother-love or a martyr complex or both.

Marabel Morgan wrote *The Total Woman* because she was

desperate about her husband's bossiness and was aware of the miserable quality of many other modern marriages. Unfortunately, her suggestion for curing modern woman's cheated feelings is to deepen her sense of submission and self-sacrifice. For the moment, her solution seemed to work for many upper-middle-class women, because at least she made them feel better about sex. She made them feel that going all out to be desirable and going all out in the enjoyment of sexual experience is all right for the Christian wife—and that's a vast improvement over the Victorian prudery which formerly governed the attitudes of many Christians. But what is to become of unattractive women or poor women? The purchase of sexy negligees may spark the marriages of women as young, beautiful, and rich as Marabel Morgan, but that solution is hardly satisfactory for families living below the poverty line or for women who would simply look ridiculous in nothing but a garter belt and black stockings.

Even more serious is the fact that what Marabel Morgan taught is nothing short of idolatry, the *worship* of the husband. She wrote, "It is only when a woman surrenders her life to her husband, reveres and worships him, and is willing to serve him, that she becomes really beautiful to him."[5] Clearly this is religious language. It is to God alone that we are to surrender our lives. God alone should be revered and worshiped.

It would be hard to say which member of the marriage would be more damaged by following *Total Woman* advice. Since I Peter 3:7 warns that a man's prayers will be hindered if he fails to give proper respect to his wife, the husband who allows his wife to worship him lives on the edge of a spiritual precipice: Sooner or later he will forget his own human limitations. On the other hand, his wife has vastly oversimplified her relationship to God. All she must do to please God is to please her husband. Her life is rendered very neat. Her husband must assume all moral responsibility, and if all goes well she will never need to doubt or struggle concerning

God's will for her life. Her husband's will is God's will. As far as moral and spiritual decisions are concerned, she can stay in a perpetual childhood—but it will be a *fun* childhood, since sex is not only permitted but encouraged!

As a matter of fact, so much did the apostle Paul *disapprove* of the idea that men and women might seek to please each other rather than concentrate on pleasing God that he expressed his personal preference that Christians should remain unmarried.

> I would like you to be free from concern. An unmarried man is concerned about the [Sovereign's] affairs—how he can please [God]. But a married man is concerned about the affairs of this world—how he can please his wife—and his interests are divided. An unmarried woman or virgin is concerned about [the Sovereign's] affairs: Her aim is to be devoted to the [Sovereign] in both body and spirit. But a married woman is concerned about the affairs of this world—how she can please her husband. I am saying this for your own good, not to restrict you. I want you to live in a right way in undivided attention to the [Sovereign God]. (I Corinthians 7:32–35 NIV)

It is interesting to notice that the apostle Paul assumes that married men, far from sitting back and allowing their wives to sacrifice their own interests in worship of the male, will be just as eager to please their wives as their wives are eager to please them! Here as elsewhere, Paul assumes a basically egalitarian relationship through mutual submission and service (see also I Corinthians 7:4). I quote the passage not in order to encourage singleness, although that certainly is a Christian life-style which ought to be more highly respected than it has previously been. Instead, I quote the passage as a reminder of how far we have departed from the Christian way of relating if and when we make husband-pleasing the be-all and end-all of a Christian wife's existence. By implication, of course, we encourage the husband to please nobody but himself.

Other fundamentalist books have gone even beyond Mrs. Morgan's in the direction of idolatry. For instance, Judith M. Miles recently wrote a book entitled *The Feminine Principle: A Woman's Discovery of the Key to Total Fulfillment*. In this book "the feminine principle" turns out to be a "pleasure principle." Says Mrs. Miles, "God has equipped me for pleasing in unique ways, and . . . many of my capacities for pleasing are clustered in the traits that we call feminine." Women, she argues, are "incarnate models of submission and loyalty." Without women to submit to them, males will never be able to understand "how to submit themselves to the mastery of God."[6]

Every time a baby girl is born, Mrs. Miles tells us, "a new incarnate picture of the human soul and of the human race is begun." If this baby girl grows up to be submissive and loyal to men, she will properly symbolize the bride of Christ. If instead she seeks her own fulfillment, she will symbolize "the harlot of Babylon" (p. 151). Mrs. Miles does not confront the inevitable conclusion to this line of reasoning: if girl babies picture the human soul that must learn to submit to God, then boy babies must picture divinity itself!

Although she does not really believe that men are gods, for all practical purposes within the marriage relationship they might as well be. Mrs. Miles tells us that "even though a male may be thoroughly corrupted from his potential to image God, a godly woman may still submit to him and mirror her part— the submission of a soul to God" (p. 152).

How all this works out in her own marriage is described in a revealing passage:

One day this familiar verse acquired a heightened meaning for me, "Wives be subject to your husbands, as to the Lord" (Eph. 5:22). It could not mean *that!* Not as to *the Lord!* But there it was. I was to treat my own human husband as though *he* were the Lord, resident in our own humble home. This was truly revelatory to me. Would I ask Jesus a basically maternal question such as "How are things at the office?" Would I remind the Lord that he was not driving prudently? Would I ever be in judgment over my Lord, over His taste, His opinions, or His actions? I was stunned—stunned into a new kind of submission (p. 44).

Here we have a first-class illustration of the danger of reading the Bible without attention to context. Taking Ephesians 5 out of its carefully controlled context of *mutual* submission and *mutual* loving service, Mrs. Miles views her husband as God incarnate. She can no longer ask him about his daily work. If he should happen to drive rapidly toward a cliff, she may not comment but must submit to his judgment. If he should happen to be color-blind, she cannot assist him in choosing more tasteful color combinations. And, of course, she can never ask her husband for help with the housework or the children. But judging from Christ's behavior as recorded in the gospels, Mrs. Miles would not have had to *ask* Jesus to help around the house. He would have seen what help she needed and would have volunteered his assistance!

Many other books also teach that it is biblical and proper for Christian marriages to be structured on the patriarchal principle of dominance and submission. Very popular is Helen B. Andelin's *Fascinating Womanhood*.[7] Although some Christian churches shy away from *Fascinating Womanhood* because of Andelin's Mormon background, there is an unacknowledged spin-off from the book, a course entitled "The Philosophy of Christian Womanhood," which has found acceptance in many churches.

Another very popular book that teaches the dominance-submission model is Larry Christenson's *The Christian Family*. So completely does Christenson place responsibility for the marriage on the woman that he even blames her for being energetic, bright, or spiritual if her husband happens to be less so than she!

> To be active, clever, or religious are noble qualities in a woman; but the energetic woman who holds down her husband in inactivity; the clever one who silences him and by the brilliancy of her conversation makes a show of his dull insignificance; and lastly, the religious one, who allows others to remark that her husband is less enlightened or awakened than herself, are three disgusting characters. [8]

Reading this, the poor Christian wife can only conclude that she had better stifle herself since she is responsible not only for the kind of person she is but for the kind of person her husband is and also for what other people think or say about them both. Christenson's book has been enthusiastically recommended by Dr. and Mrs. Billy Graham.

Other books which teach that the dominance-submission model is the only biblical form of marriage include *You Can Be the Wife of a Happy Husband, To Have and To Hold: The Feminine Mystique in a Happy Marriage,* and Anita Bryant's *Bless This House.* [9] Not one of these books is based on a careful study of the New Testament against its cultural background, and not one of them pays attention to the context of the passages concerning mutual submission.

Many of the books urging female submission to male headship are written by people whose common sense tells them that human beings who love each other ought to relate as friends and equals. Yet they feel torn because they think the Bible insists on a hierarchy in which the male is closer to God than the female and therefore, must rule the relationship. It is natural that such a basic conflict should cause a good deal of double-talk. For instance, in *A Woman's Worth,* Elaine Stedman admits that "only God has prior claim to every person" yet goes right on to argue that the female person must submit to the male person and that she must do so without "resentment or open hostility, pussycat manipulation, and power-plays, either overt or subtle."[10] And in *Ms. Means Myself,* Gladys Hunt recognizes that happy marriage is based on "mutuality," on a "oneness that reflects the character of God," yet insists that "the home must have order; there must be a leader"—and, of course, that the leader must be male.[11] I wonder: Has Gladys Hunt never experienced a healthy friendship in which two people work out their differences without anyone's domination, anyone's submission?

An attractive but disheartening book is Maxine Hancock's *Love, Honor and Be Free.* Hancock rightly argues for the necessity of free and open discussion: "Any marriage which is based on anything but full and free discussion of ideas, with mutual respect and mutual submission, would be quite unsatisfactory." But the only route for the woman who continues to disagree with her husband's assessment of a situation is "pleasant acquiescence," because his judgment is the absolute norm. She explains: "We do not submit to our husbands because they are gentle and kind, or good, or godly. But because they are our husbands."[12] Here again the male is absolutized into a god who need not be aware of his own sinful limitations since his wife is obliged to adjust herself to whatever may be his whim. It does not seem to occur to Mrs. Hancock that it is impossible to have genuinely "full and free discussion of ideas, with mutual respect and mutual submission" when both parties to the discussion know in advance that the die is always cast in favor of the male.

Like most of the traditionalist authors, Hancock postulates a world in which the *required* and *expected* submission of the female is always viewed compassionately by the male who then *voluntarily* rushes to show Christlike submission in return. Unfortunately, that view is overly simple from the psychological standpoint, besides being theologically unsound. As sociologist John Scanzoni has written:

> Power must always be tempered by justice or else it corrupts. . . . Who is to hold the husband accountable if not his wife? Who else can resist him when he is wrong? It is folly to assert "he is responsible to God." Bitter experience has convinced us of what the theologians call "total depravity." Kings, clergy and presidents with unchecked power become greedy and selfish and exploit others. The same is true of husbands with unchecked power.[13]

Fortunately, some Christian men are aware of the danger female subservience poses to their own spiritual growth and family happiness. Men like Paul Jewett, Wes Michaelson, and Donald Dayton are doing all they can to warn other males of the spiritual and emotional pitfalls of male supremacy. Glenn Peterson recently expressed his disgust at the dehumanizing disrespect hidden beneath Marabel Morgan's flattering and manipulative techniques. He concluded: "The Morgans may have a happy marriage. I believe, however, that any marriage based on the principles espoused in *The Total Woman* is a fundamentally unhealthy relationship and is, finally, mutually destructive."[14]

In a recent article, Barbara G. Harrison points out that female obsequiousness is based on contempt for men and ambivalence and confusion concerning them. She concludes, "Both Mrs. Andelin [author of *Fascinating Womanhood*] and Mrs. Morgan [author of *The Total Woman*] are happiness merchants who teach us not to confront our human pain and suffering directly, but to learn, through self-deception, to rejoice in our bonds and fetters, and thus to escape the travail and confusion that are an inescapable part of the human condition."[15] It is tragic that manipulation and self-deceit are being presented to the world as biblical. One of the destructive results of these books will be reinforcement of the widespread image of the Bible as a repressive book which lends itself to support of social injustice.

Perhaps the cruelest blow of all is the denial of full humanity to Christian women. For instance, Christian wives are counseled that they should "give him his freedom and accept him the way he is," even if the husband "stays out all night and gives . . . no reason."[16] Repeatedly, married women are told that they do not relate to God directly but rather through the authority of their husbands and that the wife's personal development is properly secondary to the husband's.

Above all, the Christian woman is told that any anger she feels is only sinful selfishness which must be overcome. Although her husband's anger and fear concerning what she has done are treated as normal reactions for which *she* is responsible, her own fear or anger concerning his actions can represent nothing but her own sinful selfishness. Thus, *The Total Woman* advises that if a woman feels offended and tells her husband so, "no matter what his reaction, your final step in dealing with the incident is to forgive your husband and forget the incident." *No matter what his reaction* can only mean that the husband is free to act in any furious or cruel way he wishes, while the wife must forgive and forget. H. Norman Wright provides a worthy corrective to all this: "Ignoring anger and refusing to recognize its presence is NOT HEALTHY. . . . Actually, ulcers, anxiety, headaches or depression are common results of repressing anger."[17]

Unfortunately, Wright is one of the authors who falls into double-talk because of an inner conflict between his common sense and what he thinks the Bible teaches. He agrees with Dwight Small that "there can be no true oneness except as there is equal dignity and status for both partners" (p. 10); yet he feels compelled to advocate female submission. In spite of this fundamental doubletalk, however, Wright's book is valuable for its emphasis on honest communication, including the creative communication of anger and resentment.

An evangelical minister recently told his congregation that since there is a limited supply of energy within the family and since the husband is likened to the Christ while the wife is likened only to the church, it makes sense to him that the wife must decrease so that the husband may increase. Because this is a paraphrase of what John the Baptist said about Jesus (John 3:30), the idolatry of the male is quite apparent. But even on the practical level, this is very poor advice. Any family counselor knows that in a one-to-one relationship the triumph of one person over the other brings about a loss of energy and intimacy in both of them. This fact is recognized in the common folk saying "Win an argument, lose a friend." A continual pattern of dominance and submission eventually destroys all communication and saps most of the energy out of the family unit.

The quality of sexual experience is frequently a good index of the quality of the whole marriage, and a September, 1975, *Redbook* survey of 100,000 American women identified open communication as perhaps the most basic requirement for sexual satisfaction within marriage. In such marital communication, either *both* persons win or *both* persons lose. The evangelical minister who assumes that the wife must sacrifice her energy so that the husband's energy may increase is teaching a patriarchal way of relating, a dominance and submission model that is antithetical to the teachings of the New Testament. Not surprisingly, he is also denying the realities of human experience.

Jesus taught us that the Christian way of relating is through mutual submission and mutual loving service. Such mutual concern calls for honest and creative communication, including the working out together of anger and hostility until the air is genuinely cleared. The equality that springs from love and mutual submission is an equality that does not sap energy from either partner but creates new and joyous energy in them both.

3

Is God Masculine?

During the last several years, radical feminists have been saying that if God is male, then the male is God. I had very little sympathy for such statements until I began to read the various attacks on equal-partnership marriage which were discussed in chapter 2. Reading them, I have been forced to realize that the exclusive use of male pronouns concerning God, the association of God with masculinity to the exclusion of femininity, has indeed been the cause of much idolatry. Christian women have sometimes unconsciously substituted their husbands, pastors, or other male leaders for God, while Christian men have sometimes assumed that their own opinions are beyond question. The assumption that our opinions are the absolute truth always means that we have confused ourselves with God, whether or not we are conscious of doing so.

To teach Christian couples that the husband must inevitably make the final decision and that the wife must inevitably bow to his will is to encourage such idolatry. To teach that girl babies represent the human soul, so that boy babies represent the divine, encourages girls to be passive and irresponsible and boys to be prideful and domineering. This situation is far from healthy for the human race and the Christian church.

Before we examine the biblical evidence concerning masculinity and femininity in the Godhead, it might be profitable to look at one more example of the damage which is done by surrounding God with exclusively male associations. In I Corinthians 13:12 the apostle Paul reminds himself (and us) that "now"—that is, here in this life—"now we see but a poor reflection. . . . Now I know in part" (NIV). And repeatedly the scriptures warn us not to confuse our limited concepts of God with the absolute truth: "For my thoughts are not your thoughts,/ and your ways are not my ways. / This is the very word of the [Sovereign]. / For as the heavens are higher than the earth, / so are my ways higher than your ways / and my thoughts than your thoughts" (Isaiah 55:8–9 NEB). The Bible certainly utilizes androcentric imagery concerning God, and Jesus encouraged us to call God our Father, so there cannot be anything wrong with that. The problem arises when we ignore, as we have, the *feminine* and *natural* imagery concerning God, so that gradually we forget that God-as-Father is a metaphor, a figure of speech, an implied comparison intended to help us relate to God in a personal and intimate way.

We begin to think of God as literally masculine! As a result, some churches have barred women from the priesthood with the argument that it is impossible for women to represent God the *Father* on earth or to be ministers of Jesus whose incarnation as a *male* is taken very seriously as proof that there is something more divine about the masculine than about the feminine.

Even so outstanding an author as C. S. Lewis fell into this trap. His masterpiece, *Till We Have Faces*, was written toward the end of his life, after his marriage to Joy Davidman. Davidman seems to have modified Lewis' attitude toward masculinity and femininity.[1] But before Joy Davidman's influence in his life, Lewis distinctly thought that God was masculine and that men as a whole were higher on the scale of being than women.

In his science-fiction novel *That Hideous Strength*, Lewis pictures a marital relationship between Jane and Mark Studdock which leaves no doubt that, to the mind of C. S. Lewis,

God is masculine. Although Jane is far more sensitive and more morally clearheaded than her husband, Mark, who gets himself involved with a brutally cruel organization trying to establish control over the human race, Jane must learn to be submissive to Mark. Because she recoils from Mark's insensitivity toward her, the spiritual leader in the novel (called the Director) teaches her that in her marital encounter with the masculine, she has only met the masculine on the first rung of a universal ladder which contains increasingly sharper and clearer distinctions between masculine and feminine as one ascends.

Had she remained a virgin, the Director explains to her, she could have bypassed the human male and could have gone on to "meet something far more masculine, higher up," to which she would have had to make "a yet deeper surrender."[2] But since she *has* married, she must learn to give up her pride in her encounter with the human being who is her husband.

The Director tells Jane: "You are offended by the masculine itself: the loud, irruptive possessive thing . . . which scatters the little kingdom of your primness. . . . The male you could have escaped, for it exists only on the biological level. But the masculine none of us can escape. What is above and beyond all things is so masculine that we are all feminine in relation to it" (pp. 315–16). In other words, although Lewis is too sophisticated to imagine that God is *a male*, he does assert that God is *masculine* and that masculinity is loud, irruptive, and possessive while femininity is little and prim. (Such a belief does sad things to men, who have to prove their masculinity by being loud, possessive, and violent, and to women, who have to try somehow to think small and act prim!)

Lewis says that even men must be feminine (that is, submissive) in relationship to God, but he does not suggest how men can *learn* this submission. What is to preserve the human male from pride and self-worship? Surrounded by feminine submission, how is he to learn to encounter the ultimate Masculine in humble submission? Lewis does not explain.

If we are to judge by the plot of *That Hideous Strength*, all that the husband must learn is a sentimental appreciation of his wife's virtues. But his appreciation makes no real difference to his practical behavior. As Jane Studdock approaches the cottage in which she will be reunited with Mark, her thoughts are all of humility, obedience, and sacrifice: "And she thought of children, and of pain and death" (p. 382). Meanwhile Mark waits for her with the feeling that she is too pure, too patient, too wonderful for him. Yet he has piled his clothes on a chair "so carelessly that they lay over the sill," getting damp in the night air. Obviously his new feelings toward his wife do not include trying to spare her unnecessary labor!

Earlier in the novel, when Mark Studdock was working for the archenemy of goodness, Jane Studdock was told that she must seek his permission before she could join the group living in the town of St. Anne's. This group, centered in the Director, represents the Body of Christ, the church of true believers. Although C. S. Lewis would probably have denied the belief if someone had pushed him to answer for it directly, in the terms of his plot he really has said that a married woman may not be converted to Christianity without seeking the permission of her unbelieving husband! It becomes obvious that speaking of God in exclusively masculine terms can create tragic confusion, even in the minds of intelligent people.

In the first chapter it was suggested that the Bible must be our major source if we are to learn the Christian way of relating to others. So it is time to see what the Bible says about the nature of God. For centuries Christians have thought and spoken of God in terms which exclude the feminine, so that people like C. S. Lewis have come to equate masculinity with God. Is that biblical? Or have Christians been guilty of overlooking evidence that if and when we picture God in human terms (a metaphoric process called anthropomorphism), we are supposed to image God as not only masculine but also feminine or all-inclusive?

As soon as we take a close look at the creation narrative in Genesis 1, we begin to suspect that God must somehow contain feminine as well as masculine characteristics. Genesis 1:26–27 tells us:

> Then God said, "Let us make [humanity] in our image and likeness to rule the fish in the sea, the birds of heaven, the cattle, all wild animals on earth, and all reptiles that crawl upon the earth." So God created [humanity] in [God's] own image; in the image of God [humanity was created]; male and female [God] created them. (NEB)

It is important to realize that in traditional translations the word *man* is used generically to mean "the human race." We can be sure of that from the pronouns which shift from the pronoun *he*, referring to both male and female, to the pronoun *them*, in order to make obvious that the reference throughout is to both the male and the female.

What Genesis 1 tells us is that both male and female were created in the image of God. If C. S. Lewis were right that God is masculine, then only the human male would be in the image of God; but such is not the case. Adam and Eve were created on the sixth day, both of them in the image of God, and together they were given command over the rest of creation. We will return to this in a later discussion of the creation story; for now, the important fact is that if both male and female are made in God's image, then in some mysterious way the nature of God encompasses all the traits which society labels feminine as well as all the traits society labels masculine.

Upon close examination, both Old and New Testaments bear out this insight. In ancient Israel the making of clothes was very distinctly the work of women, but Genesis 3:21

shows the Sovereign God making clothes for Adam and Eve and, for that matter, even dressing them like a mother dressing her children. And during the whole period of Israel's wanderings in the wilderness, God performed the mother role of providing both food and clothing for them: "Forty years long thou didst sustain them in the wilderness, and they lacked nothing; their clothes did not wear out and their feet were not swollen" (Nehemiah 9:21 NEB). Moses angrily reminded God that *God*, not *he*, was the mother of the Israelites (Numbers 11:12). The eleventh chapter of Hosea pictures God as a loving parent playing the maternal role by teaching Ephraim how to walk and caring for the children of Israel. Psalm 22:9 pictures God as a Jewish midwife: "But thou art he who drew me from the womb, who laid me at my mother's breast" (NEB). The same image is used in Psalm 71:6, Job 3:2, and Isaiah 66:9.

Other passages are even more explicit. In Isaiah 42:14 God is represented as saying, "Long have I lain still, / I kept silence and held myself in check; / now I will cry like a woman in labour, / whimpering, panting and gasping" (NEB). Isaiah 49:15 compares the Sovereign to a woman who cannot forget her suckling child, asserting that God is even more faithful than a mother. And Isaiah 66:13 pictures the Sovereign as saying, "As a mother comforts her son, so will I myself comfort you" (NEB). Psalm 131:1–2 speaks of learning humility before God in terms of the weaning of a child from its mother: "[Soverign One], my heart is not proud. . . . No; I submit myself, I account myself lowly, / as a weaned child clinging to its mother" (NEB).

Isaiah 46:3–4 is a passage which makes inescapably clear the fact that male pronouns about God are not intended to carry any notions of literal masculinity. Using the male pronoun, it pictures God as a midwife and a life-long nursemaid:

Listen to me, house of Jacob, / and all the remnant of the

house of Israel, / a load on me from your birth, carried by me from the womb: / till you grow old I am [the One], / and when white hairs come, I will carry you still; / I have made you and I will bear the burden, / I will carry you and bring you to safety (NEB)

If ever there was a picture of an *androgynous* God—a God who possesses both male and female characteristics—this is such a picture. The point, of course, is not that we are to see God as hermaphroditic but that we are to recognize that God transcends the limitations of human sexuality. Furthermore, there is no reason for us to assume that nurturing and tender parenting are eternally feminine traits. The authors of the Hebrew Scriptures, like most of us, associated nurturance and parenting with the mother because their society, like ours, assigned such roles almost exclusively to women. But we can now free ourselves from such stereotypes so that children may enjoy the care and prolonged attention not only of their mothers but also of their fathers

In order to reassure us about God not only as male but also as female, Jesus himself boldly pictured God as a woman. In Luke 15 it is recorded that Jesus told a set of three parables to the Pharisees and scribes who had been criticizing him for spending time with publicans and sinners. The first of these, the parable of the lost sheep, pictures God as a shepherd concerned about his or her one lost sheep even though there are ninety-nine other sheep. The third of them is the parable in which God is pictured as the loving father who welcomes back the long-lost son who has wasted his inheritance in debauchery. And sandwiched in between these two parables we find the parable of the lost coin in which God is pictured as a woman who is not satisfied until she has found her one lost silver piece, even though she had nine others. In order to feel the full impact of this image of God as a woman, we must remind ourselves of the patriarchal culture which tolerated the concept that a man's wickedness is better than a woman's goodness. Even in such a culture, so eager was Jesus to show his contemporaries that women were fully persons that he dared to speak of God in female terms.

All this suggests that we ought to re-think our doctrine of the Trinity which traditionally has been pictured as totally masculine. Some people have suggested that the nurturing Holy Spirit should be viewed as the feminine component in the Trinity. Others have suggested that the Second Person, the Son, should be viewed as the female component because of the submissive role he played in relationship to the Father. But when we return to Genesis 1:26 we see the use of a plural pronoun which suggests the entire Trinity: "Let *us* make man [that is, humanity] in *our* image," and in the next verse we learn that humanity which is made in the image of the Trinity is both male and female. Therefore, it would seem that humanity as male and female is made in the image of *every member* of the Trinity. If this is so, then *every* member of the Trinity possesses both masculine and feminine elements.

We have already seen that the First Person is referred to in both maternal and paternal terms in the Old and New Testaments. What about the other two Persons of the Trinity?

In our tendency toward creating stereotypes, our society has assumed that submission is feminine. Certainly Jesus is frequently shown in "feminine" attitudes of submission to the will of the First Person. Repeatedly Jesus emphasized that he came not to do his own will but the will of the one who sent him (Luke 2:49; John 5:30; John 12:49; and so forth). Repeatedly he emphasized that his power and glory were secondary, derived from the power and glory of the Father [and/or Mother]. For instance, John 5:19 records that Jesus told the Jews, "The [Child] can do nothing by [herself or] himself; [they] do only what [they] see the [Mother or] Father doing: what the [Mother or] Father does, the [Child] does" (NEB). For centuries women have been trained or socialized to be satellites revolving around the interests of their father, brother, or husband; and in the sense of secondariness, *derived* power, and submission, Jesus in his earthly life certainly exhibited these "female" traits.

Furthermore, Jesus did not hesitate to speak of himself in female terms, just as he did not hesitate to picture the First Person as a woman. When Jesus was mourning over the hardheartedness of his own people toward his message, he lamented, "O Jerusalem, Jerusalem, you who kill the prophets and stone those sent to you, how often I have longed to gather your children together, as a hen gathers her chicks under her wings, but you were not willing" (Matthew 23:37 NIV; cf. Luke 13:34–35). We can be sure that if there were any heresy involved in thinking of the Father and Son as possessing traits society would call feminine, Jesus would never have associated female imagery with them both.

On the other hand, it will not do to associate Jesus exclusively with the feminine. He was, after all, incarnated in a male body, and he is pictured not only in the so-called feminine roles of submission but also in the so-called masculine roles of the powerful generator, upholder, and judge of the universe (Colossians 1:16; II Thessalonians 1:7–8; and so forth). The combining of the typical Hebrew masculine and feminine sex-role characteristics in the person of Jesus creates a beautiful picture of him as the embodiment of all humanity, both male and female, who is then perfectly equipped to redeem the sins of us all, both male and female.

In this connection there is an ancient Hebrew tradition that there was an original Adam who preceded the biblical Adam. The original Adam was a perfect human being, the embodiment of the human ideal; and the tradition went that this perfect Adam would return to the world at the time of redemption.[3] The apostle Paul may have been alluding to that tradition when he wrote, " 'The first man, Adam, became an animate being,' whereas the last Adam has become a life-giving spirit" (I Corinthians 15:45 NEB). By referring to Jesus as the "last Adam," he would have stirred the remembrance of people steeped in the Jewish tradition that the original ideal Adam was supposed to return to the world in order to redeem it from failure and sin. He would thus be encouraging such people to accept Jesus, the last Adam, as their Messiah and redeemer.

At any rate, there can be no doubt as to the significance of another fact: when New Testament writers refer to the incarnation of Jesus, they do not speak of his becoming *anēr*, "male," but rather of his being *anthrōpos*, "human."[4] Since in English the one word *man* is used to mean both "male" and "mankind" or "humanity," this important distinction is lost in English translations. That loss makes it easy to associate the Savior of the world with masculinity to the exclusion of the feminine. But notice the difference of emphasis which comes about when we translate *anthrōpos* as "human being" rather than as "man":

> Therefore, just as sin entered the world through one human being *[anthrōpos]*, and death through sin, and in this way death came to all human beings [plural of *anthrōpos*], because all sinned— . . . But the gift is not like the trespass. For if the many died by the trespass of the one human being *[anthrōpos* understood], how much more did God's grace and the gift that came by the grace of the one human being *[anthrōpos]*, Jesus Christ, overflow to the many! (Romans 5:12, 15 NIV, with *human being* substituted for *man*).

In the King James and other versions, the latter verse reads that the gift of grace comes to *men* through one *man*, Jesus Christ. But this passage does not refer to *maleness;* rather, it refers to humanity—the sinfulness and the salvation which came about through human nature—both masculine and feminine human nature. The New Testament authors do not exclude women, the feminine, in their dealing with the nature of the Christ as a human being. But English translations often make it seem as if they do.

Fortunately, even English translations of John 1:14 capture the fact that Jesus is God incarnate as a *human being* rather than as a *male:* "So the Word became flesh; [it] came to dwell among us, and we saw its glory, such glory as befits the Father's [or Mother's] only [Child], full of grace and truth" (NEB). The use of the Greek word for "flesh," *sarx,* made it absolutely impossible for the translators to say that "the Word became man," which promptly would have become confused with "the Word became male." The glorious truth is that ":the Word became a human being," an embodying or tabernacling of the glory of God within the limitations of human nature, with its "male" and "female" components.

Mention of the Word, or *Logos,* in the first chapter of John, brings us to another important piece of evidence that in thinking of the Second Person of the Trinity we should not exclude the feminine. I Corinthians 1:24 refers to Christ as "the wisdom of God," while verse 30 indicates that Christ Jesus "is made unto us wisdom." These references as well as the whole concept of Jesus as the Logos or Word of God—the speech, expression, or reasoning of God—all of this connects Jesus with the Old Testament concept of Wisdom. And in the Old Testament, Wisdom is always pictured as a woman.

Proverbs 8 makes the connection between Wisdom and Jesus especially clear, since Wisdom is pictured as having existed from everlasting, from the beginning, before the earth was created (v. 23). Wisdom was "brought up" with the Sovereign and was God's daily delight, rejoicing always with God (v. 30). The finding of Wisdom is the one and only way of achieving spiritual life: "For [the one] who finds me finds life / and wins favour with the [Sovereign], / while [the one] who finds me not, hurts himself [or herself], / and all who hate me are in love with death" (Proverbs 8:35–36 NEB). We are strongly reminded of Jesus' own statement in John 14:6: "I am the way; I am the truth; and I am life; no one comes to the Father [or Mother] except by me" (NEB). Jesus, the Word of God, thus identifies himself with the Old Testament concept of Wisdom. And, remember, Wisdom is invariably personified as female!

Those who advocate wifely submission to the husband frequently make the statement that this submission does not imply any inferiority of female to male. As proof, they argue that the submission of the Son to the Father does not indicate that the Son was *inferior* to the Father but only that during the Son's earthly mission, he voluntarily made himself obedient to the will of the Father. And that, of course, is where this whole segment of the traditionalist argument breaks down. As we saw in chapter 1, nobody who is concerned with the Christian way of relating is going to argue against voluntary mutual submission and service. But to argue that the wife must submit to a husband who must not in turn submit to her is to argue against the mainstream of the New Testament.

It is true that Jesus voluntarily emptied self of divine glory and voluntarily submitted to the will of the First Person. It is also true that Christian wives are to submit themselves to their own husbands in the Lord. And it is equally true that Christian husbands are to empty themselves of all their private ego-strivings and to give up their beings *to* and *for* their wives, just as Jesus gave up self on behalf of the church.

The model of Jesus' relationship to the First Person during his earthly life is a model which teaches the equality of male and female, since both First and Second Persons contain feminine elements and since they are pictured repeatedly as *one* (John 10:30, for instance). In the same way, husband and wife are pictured as *one*, and the human race, made up of males and females, is ideally going to be made *one* in the Christ-nature (Galatians 3:28). First-century people understood very clearly that when Jesus claimed to be doing the work of God his Source, he was claiming *equality* with God: "For this reason [religious leaders] tried all the harder to kill him; not only was he breaking the Sabbath, but he was even calling God his own Father [or Mother], *making himself equal with God*" (John 5:18 NIV; emphasis mine). And the response of the First Person to the voluntary submission of Jesus was immediate exaltation. Because Jesus submitted to the death of the cross, "therefore God exalted [Jesus] to the highest place / and gave [Jesus] the name that is above every name" (Philippians 2:9 NIV). So if we are going to talk about the relationship between the First and Second Persons as a model for Christian wives and husbands, we are talking about a model of complete unity and equality, involving only a voluntary submission and a voluntary exaltation which is to be an example for both males and females.

The more carefully we study the Bible, the more we notice that both God the First Person and God the Second Person are frequently identified with the feminine as well as with the masculine. It therefore becomes much easier to understand the statement of Genesis 1 that both male and female are created in the image and likeness of God. But what about the Third Person of the Trinity, the Holy Spirit?

In Hebrew the word *ruach* means both "wind" and "spirit."[5] Like the word for "wisdom" *(hôkmah),* the Hebrew word for "spirit" is feminine in gender, while the New Testament Greek word for "spirit," *pneuma,* is neuter and therefore sexless.[6] The spirit or wind of Yahweh broods or sweeps over the waters at the time of creation (Genesis 1:2), and that is only one of many references to the spirit of God which help to bind together the New Testament concept of the Holy Spirit with the Old Testament concept of God (see Isaiah 11:2 and Joel 2:28–29 for other outstanding examples). Of course, these references strengthen the Christian belief in the Trinity. Because the word for *wind* or *spirit* is feminine in Hebrew and neuter in Greek, it has seemed right to some commentators to regard the Holy Spirit as the most likely candidate for the feminine component in the Trinity.

As we have already discussed, however, Genesis 1:26–27 seems to imply that both male and female were made in the image of *all three* Persons of the Trinity and, therefore, that all three of those Persons must be thought of as encompassing both male and female characteristics. The Holy Spirit is no exception. John 14:16 and 26 picture the Holy Spirit in the stereotypically feminine role of comforter, while Acts 2:3–4 associates the Holy Spirit with the masculine symbol of a flame of fire. And, of course, the Spirit is associated with a dove in Matthew 3:16, Mark 1:10, Luke 3:22, and John 1:32— and possibly also with Noah's dove (Genesis 8:8–12). Christian art ususally symbolizes the Holy Spirit as a dove surrounded with flames of fire, combining the biblical images and reminding us that in the Orient, the dove is the emblem of generation and animal heat.

Biblical imagery of the Spirit as dove is especially interesting because the dove is an androgynous symbol, a symbol combining female and male elements. Birds are regarded as masculine symbols; therefore, as a bird, the dove is symbolically masculine. But the cooing and gentleness of the dove also give it associations of great tenderness and, therefore, of femininity.[7] In pagan mythology doves were the emblems of the great love goddesses; so the dove has associations which are feminine as well as masculine. And John 3:5–8 distinctly pictures the Spirit as giving birth: "Unless [people are] born of water and the Spirit, [they] cannot enter the [realm] of God" (NIV). Since Jesus speaks these words, the New Testament shows us Jesus' association of feminine images with all three Persons of the Trinity: the Father as the woman with the lost coin, the Son as a mother hen, and the Spirit as the spiritual mother.

Therefore, we are assured that the Holy Ghost, like the Father and the Son, possesses feminine as well as masculine characteristics. We are, then, wrong to allow ourselves to imagine that God is literally masculine. It is vital that we remind ourselves constantly that our speech about God, including the biblical metaphors of God as our Father and all the masculine pronouns concerning God, are figures of speech and are not the full truth about God's ultimate nature. But on the other hand we would be no more accurate to assume that God is really our Mother than to assume literal fatherhood. The point is not that God is female, nor that God is literally a combination of male and female (androgynous), but rather that God transcends all human limitations, including the limitations of human sexuality. As Jesus told the woman of Samaria, "God is spirit, and [God's] worshipers must worship in spirit and in truth" (John 4:24 NIV). Old Testament authors attempt constantly to teach us not to associate God with human limitations, including human sexuality—by prohibiting graven images and cultic acts and by stressing the exalted oneness of God, "whose name is holy, who lives for ever" (Isaiah 57:15 NEB). When we have corrected our erroneous sexual stereotyping, we will no longer need to speak of androgyny in either God or human beings.

But at the moment, we are caught in serious problems of stereotypes which overvalue the masculine and devalue the feminine. Something must, therefore, be done about the language we use in church liturgies, private prayers, and hymns and sermons. Must we start to call God our Mother as well as our Father? Must we call Christ the daughter as well as the son of God?

Those who are insisting that God be referred to in female as well as male terms are doing so in order to sensitize us to the fact that by coming to think of God as literally masculine, we have forgotten that biblical metaphors are only metaphors. And thinking of God as masculine has serious practical consequences, as we saw in our discussion of C. S. Lewis and earlier of books like *The Total Woman* and *The Feminine Principle*.

Some people have reacted very angrily to the idea of introducing feminine aspects into Christian God-language. For instance, an editorial in the January 2, 1976, issue of *Christianity Today* implies that the authority of the Bible is at stake in such usage: "To suggest that Jesus might be called 'daughter' rather than 'son' is to denigrate the revelation of God itself and to refuse to face the fact that God chose to manifest himself as true man. Jesus was not a woman" (p.22). In the first place, *Christianity Today* misrepresents feminists by saying they want to call Jesus God's daughter *rather than* his son. The plea is that the "feminine" components in Jesus' human nature be recognized *along with* the "masculine" components. (And, of course, in patriarchal cultures, no incarnation of God in the flesh of a woman would have received a moment's serious notice!) God was incarnated in *human* flesh, as we have seen. Perhaps that is why the Bible does not make any mention of Jesus' marrying, even though it was considered a religious duty for a Jewish male to marry. It is the full *humanity* of Jesus which is stressed in the New Testament, never his maleness.

It might serve to remind us of the metaphoric nature of God-language if we followed the biblical practice of picturing God in feminine terms every once in a while. But it would serve no real purpose to switch completely to feminine pronouns and feminine references, because not only would we have to rewrite the Bible, but after a while we might forget all over again and begin to think of God as literally female. The big task is to achieve the balance of remembering that God's ways are not our ways, that as human beings we operate under all sorts of creaturely limitations, and that God the Creator is limited by *none* of them, including the limitations of human gender.

Still, we can try to achieve a healthier balance in our

religious language by speaking inclusively whenever possible. There is no reason to exclude Christian women by referring to all Christians as *sons* of God or as *brothers*. Surely there is room for daughters and sisters in the family of God! And it is remarkable how often, when we really try, it is possible to think and speak of God in orthodox ways which do not call up specifically masculine or feminine images. For instance, we can learn to address God sometimes as our Maker or Sustainer or Creator or Redeemer or Divine Friend or Liberator.

Let me give some examples of how our hymns may be made more inclusive. In that beautiful modern hymn, "They'll Know We are Christians By Our Love," the third stanza is marred by the use of the word *man* in a way which ignores women: "And we'll guard each *man's* dignity and save each *man's* pride." The fact that *man* is used in a very individual way ("*each* man"), not in a generic way, does indeed exclude women. And while it is certainly important to guard male dignity and pride, through the centuries it has been *female* dignity and pride which have taken an even greater beating. The hymn is easily made inclusive by substituting the word *one:* "And we'll guard each one's dignity and save each one's pride."

In the Doxology, wouldn't it be possible to repeat "Praise God" three times in order to avoid the male pronoun? Very frequently it is possible to avoid male connotations simply by using the noun *God* rather than using the pronoun: "In every change *God* faithful will remain"; "God Leadeth Me"; and "Just when I need God, Jesus is near . . . just when I need God most." And surely, in "Faith of Our Fathers," it would be not only possible but absolutely beneficial to alternate *Mothers* and *Fathers* when singing the various stanzas, since foremothers as well as forefathers endured dungeons and prisons dark, and foremothers even more than forefathers took the gospel to other nations and preached the faith "by kindly words and virtuous life."

Sometimes hymns can be made more inclusive simply by switching to the plural: "*They* who would valiant be . . . Let *them* in constancy / Follow the Master." There is a slight problem here, since the "avowed intent" of "he who would valiant be" is "to be *a* pilgrim"; but it is possible to think of a group of people each making an individual internal vow, so it is not illogical to sing of "*their* first avowed intent / To be a pilgrim."

"Once to every man and nation" might become "Once to every mind and nation / Comes the moment to decide." "Rise up, O Men of God" is easily changed to "Rise up, People of God." And perhaps all of us owe to ourselves the experience of singing all three stanzas of "This Is My Father's World" as "This Is My Mother's World," complete with female pronouns, just to get a sense of the freshness of it all. The extent of the displacement we feel during this or similar exercises will give us an accurate index of just how much our unconscious mind remains confused about the maleness of God. We might also try out on ourselves Mary Daly's phrase "the sisterhood of man." After all, if *man* is truly generic, the *sisterhood of man* is every inch as logical as *brotherhood of man*. If it doesn't feel that way to us, then we are forced to admit that the word *man* has male connotations for us rather than genuinely inclusive ones.

Modifying our hymns and forms of addressing God and our references to God will require effort. Some of us may feel dissatisfied with this effort, since new language patterns always feel uncomfortable at first. But if the changes remove artificial barriers which are keeping certain people away from the Christ, and free us from the erroneous assumption that God is masculine, and stop us from oppressing one sex and idolizing the other on the basis of that assumption, then the effort will be worthwhile.

4

Freedom from Stereotypes

What are little girls made of? Sugar and spice and every-thing nice. What are little boys made of? Snakes and snails and puppy-dog tails.

Aside from the delight that children feel in the presence of rhyme and rhythm, they are getting a message from that familiar nursery rhyme. While at first it may seem that girls get the best end of things, it takes only a little reflection to realize the kind of pressure which is exerted by telling people that they are made of "everything nice." In other words, little girls learn that they are intended to give delight, while little boys learn that they have no particular responsibility to give delight. Little boys may function in individualistic ways which may even sometimes be frightening or repulsive to other people, since little boys are made from snakes and snails. But little girls should not behave in disturbing ways, for they are supposed to be pleasant to the taste of other people, like sugar and spice. This type of learning, which surrounds a child in preschool years and all the way through school, is called socialization.

Have you ever noticed your own discomfort when you are shown a baby whose gender you are not sure of? You feel afraid to make any distinct reaction, because you know deep inside yourself that the parent would be distressed should you contribute to the wrong type of socialization. If the baby is a girl, you wouldn't want to pretend to sock her little tummy and call her a real he-man! If the baby is a boy, you wouldn't want to admire his curls and talk about the loveliness of his skin! Almost from the moment of birth, the socialization process begins.

In her science-fiction novel *The Left Hand of Darkness*, Ursula Le Guin describes an imaginary planet where people spend most of their lives in a state which is neither one sex nor the other.[1] Only during certain periods of sexual desire (called "kemmer") do they become sexual beings. An individual never knows, right up until kemmer begins, which sex he/she will become this time. After the time of kemmer, he/she returns to the neither/nor state until the next period of sexual experience, during which he/she may become once again the same sex as before or may just as likely spend some time as the other sex. Consequently, a single individual during one lifetime may become the mother of several children and the father of several others.

All of this may seem very confusing and unattractive to us. The important factor for our purposes is the extreme discomfort felt by the normal male observer from Terran (Earth) in the presence of such individuals. How would *you* feel in the presence of somebody who looks like a rather sexless person but is known to be the mother of several children and the father of several others and who just may blossom into a sensual woman next week—or may just as likely become a sensual male? What you would feel would probably be a more intense version of the discomfort you feel in the presence of a baby whose gender you do not know. It's bad enough not to know how to react to a baby; it's worse not to know how to react to an adult. Our socialization has taught us that we must have one set of reactions for women, another set of reactions for men. What has been overlooked in our socialization is the importance of being able to react to one another simply as persons, as human beings.

Our socialization has not emphasized the fact that a male and female human being have far more in common with each other than either of them has with any other organic being. A human male has far more in common with a human female than he has with a stallion or a bull. Although we Americans claim that we belong to the Judeo-Christian tradition, we have forgotten to stress that the male and female human being are both made in the image of God. The horses and cows and all the other animals, no matter how beautifully complex, do not share in that image. The human race is, therefore, held responsible for all the rest of creation.

Our socialization has emphasized the differences between men and women to such a tremendous degree that it has obscured some of the basic meanings of the Genesis creation stories. The reason Genesis 2 pictures God as creating woman out of the rib of Adam instead of out of another handful of dust is surely to emphasize that male and female are far more closely similar to each other than to anything else in creation. In the process of naming the animals, we are told, Adam saw many females of many species; but he knew that none of them was suitable for him. On the other hand, the moment he saw woman, he recognized her as "bone from my bones, flesh from my flesh." The socialization process which emphasizes radical differences between male and female is therefore a denial of the oneness of the human race as taught in Genesis. According to this basic Judeo-Christian source, our humanity in the image of God is far more central than the biological distinctives which make us physically different from each other.

Because of the role socialization to which we have all been subjected, we assume that certain characteristics are "masculine" and certain characteristics are "feminine." Men, we assume, are naturally more aggressive, rational, and competitive than women. Women are naturally more passive, romantic, and supportive than men. Men lead, women follow. Men who fail to be dominant are lacking in true masculinity. Women who fail to be quietly dependent are lacking in true femininity. These assumptions are known as sex role stereotypes. Of course they lead to stereotyped expectations about male and female performance in the world. Men should be the bosses, women the secretaries. Men should be active in the business world, while women's place is in the home. Men should be up front, women behind the scenes.

Even psychologists have been subjected to this socialization, so that until very recently most of them have assumed that healthy women differ from healthy men by being more submissive, less independent, less adventurous, more easily influenced, less aggressive, less competitive, more excitable in minor crises, more easily hurt, more emotional, more conceited about appearance, less objective, and less interested in math and science. And it is not surprising that such characteristics should often surface in women who have been taught from the beginning of their lives that proper little girls are made of sugar and spice and everything nice. When one little girl told former President Nixon that she wanted to enter politics, he promptly assured her that what she *really* wanted was to become a wife and mother—and that is typical of the kind of pressure toward conformity which each sex is made to feel.

For little boys, serious problems arise if their personalities happen to be fairly shy, passive, and retiring. Although girls are permitted to be tomboys when they are small, there is no positive or even *tolerant* term for little boys who want to play with dolls and who prefer solitary or nonaggressive pastimes. For women, the problem becomes exceptionally serious in young adulthood because the usual psychological description of a normal woman—submissive, dependent, easily influenced, and so forth—is actually the profile of a neurotic person.[2] Psychologist Joyce Brothers comments that it is "no wonder women are perplexed and bewildered," since "to ask a healthy personality to fit herself into a neurotic pattern is indeed enough to drive a woman crazy."[3] In exactly this fashion, thousands of women are driven into depressions or heart palpitations or other psychogenic illnesses by trying to make themselves fit into social expectations which run counter to their own personalities and gifts.

The young man who tends to be dependent or passive can at least tell himself that he is a snail or perhaps a friendly puppy-dog tail instead of a snake. But there is no such "out" for the assertive female leader who offends people because they assume she should confine herself to being "everything nice." If a male is logical and powerful in the presentation of evidence, he is admired for his strength; if a woman if equally logical and powerful in the presentation of evidence, she is often criticized for being tough, a "shrew."

According to several prominent sociologists and medical researchers, the scientific evidence indicates that masculine and feminine identity is far more dependent on social learning than on genetic makeup. For instance, studies by John Money and Anke Ehrhardt show that although a certain hermaphrodite—that is, a person born with both male and female organs—may actually be female as far as chromosomes and hormones are concerned, she may still be successfully brought up as either a boy or a girl, depending upon the sex which is assigned to the child by other people. A boy trained for any reason to think of himself as a girl would grow up acting like a girl; a girl trained to think of herself as a boy would grow up acting like a boy. The only logical conclusion is that "the physiological differences between the sexes do not in themselves determine the dissimilarities in thinking and behavior. *Learning* makes the difference."[4]

Some people argue that masculinity and femininity are inborn or innate and that it is "natural law" or "God's will" that the sexes be as different as possible from each other in order to preserve their separate roles. Such a notion runs counter to scientific evidence and denies the oneness emphasized in the biblical accounts of creation. Furthermore, if masculinity and femininity were created by God or built into natural law, so that never the twain should meet (except in intercourse), then social expectations toward male and female should be uniform in every culture all over the world. Such is not the case. For instance, one study of selected cultures found that in 12 societies, it is expected that men should always carry the heavy burdens, while in 57 other societies it is expected that women should always carry the heavy burdens. In 158 societies it is expected that women should always do the cooking, but in 5 societies it is understood that cooking is exclusively a man's job. In 95 societies the manufacture and repair of clothing is only done by women, but in 12 other societies this work is done only by men. In 14 societies, houses are always built by women, but in 86 other societies, housebuilding is exclusively a male prerogative.[5]

To take a specific example: on Cheju Island off the coast of Korea, the women work for the family living while the men stay at home and care for the children. Isolated on this small island in the Yellow Sea, the population (about 60,000) had escaped outside influences for thousands of years until the recent invasions of tourists—and until recently both men and women on Cheju Island have been contented with the way things were.[6]

Anthropologist Margaret Mead has shown that in certain New Guinea tribes, the ideal temperament for men and women differed drastically from one tribe to another. In one tribe, the ideal for both sexes was gentleness. In another tribe, the ideal for both sexes was aggressiveness. In a third tribe, the ideal for males was dependence and affectionate sensitivity, while the ideal for females was aggressive dominance.[7]

With a background of such knowledge, we can begin to realize that our own society's masculine ideal of rationality, dominance, and so forth, and our feminine ideal of emotion, submission, and so forth, are little more than localized "tribal" assumptions, passed on from generation to generation by the process called socialization. Far from being God's ideal or a universal natural law, our rigid sex role stereotypes may often block individuals from developing into all that they were meant to be.

But doesn't the Bible teach that women should be gentle and modest and self-effacing? And if it does, then isn't our socialization process correct? Wouldn't the New Guinea tribes that teach women to be aggressive be simply *wrong?*

It is indeed true that the Bible instructs women to be modest, patient, and humble. For instance, I Peter 3:3–4 urges Christian women to behave modestly and to be concerned not so much with external adornments as with their "inner self, the unfading beauty of a gentle and quiet spirit, which is of great worth in God's sight" (NIV). But the Bible also instructs Christian *males* to be modest, patient, and humble!

For instance, the very context of the I Peter passage about a woman's inner beauty teaches that "it is commendable if a man bears up under the pain of unjust suffering because he is conscious of God. . . . If you suffer for doing good and you endure it, this is commendable before God" (I Peter 2:19–20 NIV). And Titus 2 teaches men and women, young and old, that we all should "live self-controlled, upright and godly lives," citing patience and temperateness and love as some of the specific advice to *male* Christians. The famous thirteenth chapter of I Corinthians defines love as being patient, kind, unselfish, and long-suffering; and love is identified as the greatest of all the spiritual gifts, the ideal for Christian men as well as Christian women.

So once again it becomes evident that our culture has gone wrong by teaching submissive Christian virtues only to women and failing to teach the same ideals to men. It would seem that the New Guinea tribe which perceives gentleness as the ideal temperament for both men and women comes closer to the biblical ideal than the dominance and submission pattern which has been practiced for centuries in the so-called Christian nations!

But if everyone in the culture were humble, patient, and loving, where would we get our leaders? Here I think it is important to distinguish between aggression and assertion, between dominance and firm leadership. Aggressiveness is characterized by militant, forceful attitudes and actions which are intended to dominate and master other people. Assertiveness is characterized by positive affirmation and firm insistence on the individual's perceptions in the face of denial or rejection. The goal of assertiveness is usually to bring about recognition of the viewpoint of the asserter, as opposed to gaining mastery over someone else's personality. A leader must be assertive but need not be aggressive. Aggressive persons tend to push and shove; assertive people do not push and shove others, but neither do they stand silent while others push and shove them, if there is anything that can possibly be done about it.

Most American males have been taught to be assertive and even aggressive by the socialization process we have been discussing. But many women are in need of assertiveness training. This need not be in violation of biblical injunctions toward mutual submission and mutual service, since healthy human relating requires that each member of a relationship communicate or assert his or her honest feelings to the other person. Patience and self-control do not require the cultivation of a doormat mentality! It is true that Jesus was passive and submissive at the crucifixion, for a very specific purpose and to achieve a supreme goal; but he was aggressive with the money-changers in the temple and was extremely assertive in his many confrontations with the self-righteous religious leaders of his day. His example demonstrates that self-sacrifice is right only when the sacrifice is freely chosen to bring about a good greater than that which is given up; that even aggressiveness may be called for in rare and unusual circumstances; and that assertiveness is frequently necessary.

Sociologists use the word *instrumental* to identify the characteristics associated with the socialization of boys, and *expressive* to identify the characteristics associated with the socialization of girls. Instrumental behaviors are related to getting a job done: activity, assertiveness, dominance, self-reliance, achievement orientation, and emotional control. On the other hand, expressive behaviors are people-oriented: emotional responsiveness, affection, nurturance, and concern for interpersonal relationships. As we have seen, the Bible pictures all three Persons of the Trinity as manifesting not only instrumental, so-called masculine traits but also expressive, so-called feminine traits. And the Bible tells us that as human beings we are all made in the image of God. In order to become fully human, therefore, we all need to cultivate all the desirable human qualities which are consonant with our individual personalities, without worrying about whether they are stereotypically associated with our particular sex.

Damage is done to the human spirit by assigning valuable qualities to one sex exclusively. To teach boys to be exclusively instrumental or task-oriented is to rob them of their opportunity to be tender, open about their feelings, and in touch with the full range of human emotion. To teach girls to be exclusively expressive is to rob them of the opportunity to achieve worthwhile career goals and a sense of their independent worth. Traits which the Bible identifies as the enemies of full humanity, such as domineering over another person, should not be taught to *either* sex; but traits which are valuable in either sex are part of the human potential and should not become exclusively the property of either half of the human race.

Will this lead to unisex? Of course not. Unisex is the state of being physically indistinguishable by hair or clothing as either male or female. It is possible for a person to be dressed in unisex fashion and to exhibit the worst sex-role stereotypes in words and actions. And it is possible to be clearly identifiable as male or female while developing one's full range of talents in a rich and satisfying lifestyle.

Unisex is no more desirable than any other attempt at total conformity. What I am describing is the opposite of conformity: the full development of each person's God-given talents and personality traits in all their infinite variety. Since every Person of the Trinity is biblically pictured both in "masculine" instrumental and "feminine" expressive terms, we need have no fear about developing all aspects of our own individual potential. To put fancy terms on it, since the Holy Trinity is pictured as androgynous, we need not fear to be psychologically androgynous as well. Biologically we remain male and female and relate to each other in that fashion; but we are basically *persons* and need to develop whatever gifts we have been granted, without undue concern about whether society brands those gifts as "masculine" or "feminine."

But will psychological androgyny lead to increased homosexual activity, as some people fear? All the evidence points in the opposite direction. In her study of the tribes which regard either gentleness or aggressiveness as the single temperamental norm for *both* sexes, Margaret Mead found no evidence of homosexual activity. But in societies where sex-role differentiation is extremely rigid, such as in an Arab culture like Libya, homosexual activity is widespread. The reason for this is that when men and women are taught to regard each other as totally different and radically unlike, the only reason for them to get together is for sexual intercourse. Consequently when people want to develop tender intimacy with a like-minded person, they may be drawn to someone of their own sex rather than to the radically different other sex. Where orientation allows, tender intimacy may lead into sexual expression. Thus the average Libyan male will use women for sexual intercourse, for all practical purposes raping the women in his harem without any foreplay or tenderness; but he will often reserve his genuine intimacy and affectionate sexuality for his male friends. Here again we see the significance of the Genesis creation narratives; they demonstrate the essential unity of the human race and the possibility of like-mindedness and one-fleshedness despite male-female distinctives. By emphasizing psychological androgyny and breaking free from sex-role stereotyping, we will not be encouraging homosexual activity. Rather, we will be alleviating certain conditions that might push bisexual people toward homosexual experience.

Males and females are intended to work in harmonious partnership in society, in the home, and in the church. When men reject their so-called female component, they become contemptuous of the other sex as well. Instead of manifesting the best qualities of what society calls feminine, such as tenderness, intuitiveness, and nurturance, they develop the negative qualities, such as narcissism and selfishness. And when women reject their so-called masculine component, they also become contemptuous of the other sex. Instead of developing the better traits of what society terms masculine, such as strength and assertiveness and clear logic, they tend to develop the negative qualities of that "masculine" component, such as opinionatedness and rigid dogmatism.

Of course, all this escalates the war of the sexes. By contrast, as we have seen, the Bible teaches mutual concern and mutual respect, for "woman is not independent of man, nor is man independent of woman. For as woman came from man, so also man is born of woman. But everything comes from God" (I Corinthians 11:11–12 NIV). This implies that marriage is a partnership of equals under God. And in witness that "everything comes from God," Christian communities should be characterized by harmonious relationships between men and women, so that fully qualified women as well as men are acceptable in all aspects of Christian ministry and church governance. Only then will Christian churches be true to the biblical teaching that male and female are made in the image of a God who is both paternal and maternal, both powerful and submissive, both instrumental and expressive, both transcendent (above us) and immanent (within us).

When the apostle Paul wrote Galatians 3:28, his dazzling vision of a society without barriers between Jew and Greek, between slave and free, between male and female, this was probably his meaning. Certainly he could not have meant that those born Jews and those born Gentiles would lose their ethnic roots. According to the context, he meant that those recent rules and practices which militated against the Gentile converts, forcing them to conform to Jewish stereotypes, would be abolished in the equality of Christian fellowship (Galatians 2:14). Similarly, he could not have meant that Christian males and females would lose their biological distinctives, but rather that in the freedom and psychological wholeness fostered by Christian fellowship, each male and each female would be free to develop his or her gifts without reference to gender-based stereotypes. They would not be forced to conform to sexual stereotyping any more than Gentile converts would be forced to conform to Jewish religious customs.

When we compare these biblical insights with the findings of recent psychological research, we find a remarkable positive correlation. For instance, Sandra Lipsitz Bem describes some of the practical effects of sex-role stereotyping in an interesting article called "Fluffy Women and Chesty Men." She describes six different carefully controlled psychological experiments, the results of which all pointed to the same conclusion: "traditional concepts of femininity and masculinity do restrict a person's behavior in important ways." Dr. Bem explains that "in a modern complex society like ours, an adult has to be assertive, independent and self-reliant," but "traditional femininity makes many women unable to behave in these ways." Futhermore, " an adult must also be able to relate to other people, to be sensitive to their needs and concerned about their welfare, as well as to be able to depend on them for emotional support." But Dr. Bem's research indicates that "traditional masculinity keeps men from responding in such supposedly feminine ways."

Dr. Bem finds the psychological ideal in androgyny which "allows an individual to be both independent and tender, assertive and yielding, masculine and feminine." People identified as androgynous on psychological tests tended to excell stereotypically masculine men or feminine women in overall intelligence, in spatial ability, and in creativity. Androgynous women were just as warmly responsive to babies as were the feminine women, but the androgynous women were far more playful than either the feminine women or masculine men. Dr. Bem concludes that psychological androgyny will permit people "to cope more effectively with diverse situations."[8]

Similar corroboration of biblical insights occurs in the research reported by psychologist Robert Ornstein. He explains that the two hemispheres of the human brain are "specialized for different modes of information-processing." The left hemisphere, which governs the right side of the body, operates primarily in a verbal, intellectual, sequential mode. The right hemisphere, which governs the left side of the body, operates primarily in a spatial, simultaneous mode. The right hemisphere mode, Ornstein explains, is often "devalued by the dominant, verbal intellect." The right hemisphere appears inelegant and lacks the formal reasoning power of the more polished intellectual left hemisphere. Because the right hemisphere is more involved in space than time and more involved in intuition than in logic and language, it is frequently forgotten and ignored, especially in scientific education and practice. But Ornstein thinks that the right-hemisphere mode may well prove to be essential for science and even for the survival of civilization.[9]

Although Ornstein does not link these findings to sexual attitudes, it does not take much effort to remember that throughout Western literature and society, the female has been associated with the exotic, mysterious, and intuitive approach to reality (the right hemisphere so devalued by modern society). And the male has been associated with analytic thinking, formal logic, and verbal intellect (the left hemisphere which has been given almost exclusive respect in the sciences and in popular attitudes).

By urging a more equal use of the two basic modes of consciousness, the logical and the intuitive mode, Dr. Ornstein lends support to our contention that a total split between what is "properly feminine" and "properly masculine" is harmful both to the individual and to society as a whole. It is time to stop categorizing individual traits. It is time for men to develop those aspects of themselves which are considered "feminine" and for women to develop those aspects of themselves which are considered "masculine"—without fear. God has given us whatever gifts we possess. We dare not refuse to develop them out of fear of human rejection. We must learn to listen to the voice of God, even when that voice runs counter to social stereotypes.

Viennese psychologist Otto Rank once remarked that "woman had to be made over by man in order to become acceptable to him."[10] And in the process of remaking women into submissive and dependent creatures who would be no threat to their own self-confidence, men robbed themselves of honoring the functions of that valuable right hemisphere of their own brains. Scorning the "feminine," men devalued their own intuitive sense and their own ability to grasp situations as a whole. Thus patriarchal society has condemned itself to an overbalance of left-hemisphere thinking. In religion, the result frequently has been an overemphasis on doctrine and logic with a corresponding loss of warm emotional responses. We are currently witnessing many attempts to correct this imbalance, including the charismatic movement in many churches, the rage for astrology and the widespread interest in Transcendental Meditation and other Oriental concepts, and the emphasis on "values clarification" in education. Admittedly some people have carried their reaction to a truly anti-intellectual extreme which is no healthier than the original logic-chopping. The church as well as the school and the home will, therefore, profit from a sanely balanced appreciation of the right hemisphere's intuitions (the "feminine") working in harmonious equality with the rational left hemisphere (the "masculine"). Under such conditions, men are free to recover their souls and women are free to recover their minds.

Psychologically speaking, the Christ-nature provides the biblical symbol of wholeness and perfect physical and mental health, possessing "wisdom and stature, and . . . favor with God and humanity" (Luke 2:52 NIV). So when Paul says that *in Christ* there is oneness, there is neither male nor female, he is envisioning the breakdown of all stereotypical behavior, including the hierarchical pattern of male dominance and female submission. He is supporting the concept that a healthy personality involves a harmony between the so-called masculine and feminine components in both men and women, while a healthy society involves a harmonious sense of partnership between those who were created biologically male and those who were created biologically female. As John B. Breslin says, the reason we must correct our language about God to include feminine as well as masculine analogies is that "God is neither masculine nor feminine and *we are all both*."[11]

Obedience to the biblical standard of mutual submission combined with freedom from sex-role stereotypes will promote wholeness within the individual personality and the Christian community. Such wholeness is described in Ephesians 4:11–13; God gave "some to be apostles, some to be prophets, some to be evangelists, and some to be pastors and teachers, to prepare God's people for works of service, so that the body of Christ may be built up until we all reach unity in the faith and in the knowledge of the [Child] of God and become mature, attaining the full measure of perfection found in Christ" (NIV). Since the Bible pictures the Christ in both stereotypically masculine and feminine roles, to attain "the full measure of perfection found in Christ" is to reflect Jesus' psychological androgyny and to relate without any rigid role-playing to the members of the other sex.

For too long we Christians have ignored such implications. For too long Christian leaders have blocked genuine friendship between men and women by insisting on a pattern of dominance and submission rather than responding to the liberating message of the Good News. For too long many Christian churches have denied the fulfillment of Jesus' great prayer in John 17. This prayer takes on new dimensions in the light of a Godhead of three interrelating Persons who each contains a harmony of "masculine" and "feminine" elements. Jesus prayed "that all of them may be one, . . . just as you are in me and I am in you. May they also be in us. . . . I have given them the glory that you gave me, that they may be one as we are one: I in them and you in me. May they be brought to complete unity" (NIV). Neither male nor female, all one in the Body of the New Humanity.

5

Pauline Contradictions and Biblical Inspiration

So far we have reviewed a great deal of biblical evidence in support of male-female equality. It is now time to confront squarely the major problems posed by those who deny this position and interpret the Bible in another way. At the outset we must admit that Christian traditionalists and the most many feminists agree firmly on one point: both camps believe that the Bible supports male supremacy in homes and churches. But while the traditionalists applaud biblical support for social and sexist hierarchy, many feminists attack the Bible for the same reason: they see it as an instrument of social oppression, most notably of black people and women. There are also certain Judaic or Christian feminists who respect the Bible but who despair of finding a way to interpret it in a fashion favorable to female equality in the human race. These people are, of course, divided against themselves. They are enduring the agony of sensing injustice in the God they attempt to worship.

But there is another category of feminists, men and women who call ourselves biblical feminists, who believe that the Bible is properly interpreted as supporting the central tenets of feminism. *Webster's New Collegiate Dictionary* defines feminism as "the theory of the political, economic, and social equality of the sexes" along with "organized activity on behalf of women's rights and interests." I am using the word feminism in exactly those senses, with the understanding that what the Bible teaches as best for women will be best also for the men and children with whom they relate.

Traditionalists cite New Testament instructions about the submission of first-century wives and church women as proof that it is forever the will of God for women to remain in a subordinate role in marriage and in the church. And it is perhaps understandable that the Bible should seem to traditionalists and even to many feminists to support male supremacy. Many of the Old Testament authors assume that patriarchy is the will of God for the social order; in other words, they assume that men should have absolute power over their families, over worship, and over society in general. In the New Testament the same patriarchal assumption prevails, with several notable exceptions: Jesus' personal behavior, the ministry of certain women in the early church, the many passages concerning mutual submission, and several prophetic passages which envision the regenerative effects of the gospel on human society.

Because patriarchy is the cultural background of the scriptures, it is absolutely basic to any feminist reading of the Bible that *one cannot absolutize the culture in which the Bible was written*. To absolutize something means to regard it as the fundamental or ultimate reality. So to absolutize the biblical culture would mean to assume that the standards of ancient Israel or first-century society represent God's ultimate will for the human race. Instead of making such an assumption, we must make careful distinctions between what is "for an age" and what is "for all time." We cannot assume that because the Bible was written against the backdrop of a patriarchal social structure, patriarchy is the will of God for all people in all times and all places.

To clarify by means of a different example, most biblical authors assumed that kings ruled by divine anointing and that absolute monarchy was the divinely ordained form of government as long as direct national obedience to God was not possible. Because the king was supposed to be God's earthly representative, God was frequently spoken of in terms of kingship (Psalm 24; Jeremiah 10:7; Revelation 19:16). Yet although traditionalists insist that New Testament instructions to first-century wives and church women are normative for all times and all places and that God must be spoken of as a Father and that it is offensive and a trifle heretical to speak of God as a Mother, they do not insist on a return to absolute monarchy. And they do not require twentieth-century Americans to think and speak of God in royal terms. In other words, where political government is concerned, both feminists and traditionalists join in de-absolutizing the biblical culture. We all agree that one can be a Christian without believing in absolute monarchy. And some of us are asking that in the area of sexual politics as well as in the area of national politics, we de-absolutize the biblical culture.

Similarly, both Old and New Testament authors assume that it is the will of God for some people to be the slaves of other people; and there was a time when traditionalists argued that, for that very reason black people could justly be enslaved by whites. Fortunately there were some eighteenth- and nineteenth-century evangelicals who believed that the gospel was intended to lead to an egalitarian society in which the injustices of racism would be abolished. Partly through their efforts, emancipation triumphed; and the pro-slavery view is no longer upheld, even by traditionalists.[1]

Because the biblical cultures practiced slavery, the relationship between God and humanity is sometimes pictured as a master-slave relationship (Matthew 23:8; Ephesians 6:9; and the first verses of Romans, Philipians, Titus, James, I Peter, and Jude). But imagery of slavery and mastery is very repugnant to the modern ear. Neither traditionalists nor feminists would think of insisting that contemporary Christians refer to themselves as the slaves of God or pray to "Our Master who is in Heaven." On the subject of slavery, as on the subject of monarchy, we have de-absolutized the biblical culture. We all agree that one can be a biblical Christian without believing in slavery. In fact, most of us, even traditionalists, would go further and say that enslaving other people is a practice *antithetical* to genuine Christianity. Here again, what biblical feminists are asking is that as in the area of slavery and that of absolute monarchy, we be *consistent* about de-absolutizing the biblical culture. We ask that modern Christians concern themselves with fulfilling the visions of a society regenerated by the power of the gospel instead of clinging to the sinful social order into which the gospel was first introduced.

The apostle Paul knew that the sinful social order could not be changed overnight. But he apparently glimpsed two truths concerning human society: that eventually the principles of the gospel would bring about a more egalitarian society, and that ultimately God's plan for a redeemed social order was an egalitarian one. This combined truth seems to be the point of the message to slaves and their masters in Ephesians 6:5, 9: "Slaves, obey your earthly masters with respect and fear, and with sincerity of heart, just as you would obey [the] Christ. . . . And masters, treat your slaves in the same way. Do not threaten them, since you know that [the one] who is both their Master and yours is in Heaven, and there is no favoritism with [God]" (NIV).

Masters, treat your slaves in the same way. To treat the slaves in the same way as the slaves were to treat their masters—as if they were relating to the Christ—would have brought slavery to a screeching halt. And *there is no favoritism with God:* this surely is a reminder that all people are equal in the sight of God. The implication is that those who want to reflect the nature of God here on earth should stop playing favorites and should treat one another more nearly as equals. But since Paul could not abolish slavery single-handedly and overnight, he wrote instructions to both masters and slaves which would at least alleviate the conditions of slavery until the gospel had done its full work in that area.

Paul also wrote instructions to first-century wives and husbands which closely parallel the instructions to masters and slaves. As we have seen, Paul added a subtle but distinct note of equality through mutual submission which, if followed, would have revolutionized marriage within one generation. "Wives, submit to your husbands as to the [Sovereign]. . . . Husbands, love your wives, just as Christ loved the church and gave self up for her" (Ephesians 5:22, 25 NIV). Just as slave masters were reminded that they had a Master in heaven, first-century heads of families were reminded that they had a Head in heaven (I Corinthians 11:3) and that they were to manifest Christlike self-sacrifice toward their wives. It would seem that in the case of first-century female subordination, as in the case of first-century slavery, people were being told how best to live in an established social order that could not be changed overnight. And they were being taught principles which, if obeyed, would speedily have done away with both slavery and male domination.

But at this point we must begin to face a serious problem in our interpretation of the Bible. Although the Bible is a holy book, it has come to us through human channels. And it seems apparent that some of the apostle Paul's arguments reflect his personal struggles over female subordination and show vestiges both of Greek philosophy (particularly Stoicism) and of the training he had received from his own socialization and especially from Rabbi Gamaliel. Although there are some feminists who think that all of Paul's words and attitudes can be explained in a completely harmonious egalitarian fashion once we achieve a full understanding of the cultural conditions and the Greek usage involved, to date I have not found their interpretations fully convincing.

Rabbi Gamaliel was relatively humane in his attitudes toward women, but the tradition he taught to Paul was one which favored male domination. Even in the 1970s many scholars still assumed that Genesis 2:23–24 teaches that woman was "created to serve man as a suitable helper," and that Genesis 3:16 shows that "the wife is inferior to her husband."[2] Oral and written traditions current at the times of Jesus and Paul the apostle are recorded in the Genesis Rabbah, a verse-by-verse exposition of Genesis edited about A.D. 425. This Genesis Rabbah (45:5) describes women as "greedy, eavesdroppers, lazy, and jealous . . . also querulous and garrulous." Gamaliel's own grandfather, the famous Rabbi Hillel, taught that wherever there were many women, there was much witchcraft.

Vestiges of Paul's social conditioning are implied in I Corinthians 14:34, where women "are not allowed to speak, but must be in submission, as the Law says," a reference not to the Old Testament itself but to the social customs and rules of the first-century. The Old Testament clearly *assumed* female submission but contained no law to *command* it, whereas laws and customs were developed later which *required* the subservience of women. For instance, the Talmud records that no matter how many slaves a wife is able to purchase with her dowry, her husband should still require her to serve him, because idleness leads to boredom, and boredom leads to promiscuity (Kethuboth 59b). And the wife was *required* to wash her husband's face, hands, and feet, make his bed, and pour his wine (Kethuboth 61a). Any income she earned from her own handicraft or from her premarriage assets was the property of her husband (Kethuboth 65b, 78a, 48b).[3] Paul's reference in I Corinthians 14:34 to a law which requires female silence and submission is, therefore, most probably a reference to oral traditions, especially to the tradition recorded in Megillah 23a that women should not be permitted to read from the Torah because of "the dignity of the congregation."

For Bible believers the problem is that the apostle Paul

seems to contradict his own teachings and behavior concerning women, apparently because of inner conflicts between the training he had received and the liberating insights of the gospel. Paul had positive and cordial relationships with many women who were leaders in the early church. In Romans 16 he sends greetings to Priscilla (Prisca) and Aquilla, who are such a perfect biblical model of an equal-partner marriage that they alone ought to silence all those who contend that such marriages are unbiblical. Priscilla and Aquilla made tents (Acts 18:3), and both of them were teachers of the word and active in the Lord's work, with a church meeting in their home. Both of them had risked their lives for the apostle Paul, and he writes his warm gratitude to them both (Romans 16:3–5). Paul also manifests warm personal relations with Nympha, in whose home a local congregation met for services (Colossians 4:15).[4] In Romans 16:7 Paul salutes a woman named Junia as a kinsman and a fellow prisoner and says she is "outstanding among the apostles"! And in Romans 16:1 he commends Phoebe, referring to her as both *diakonos* and *prostatis*. Paul seems perfectly comfortable with the fact that Phoebe was a minister or deacon (*diakonos*) of the church at Cenchrae and a ruler over many people (*prostatis*), including no doubt many males. He urges the Roman Christians "to give her any help she may need from you" (Romans 16:2 NIV).

So it is with great surprise that we find the same apostle Paul who manifested such cordial relationships with these female church leaders, and with other women as well, arguing for female subordination in the Corinthian church on the basis of the second chapter of Genesis. In I Corinthians 11:7–9 Paul argues that women must have covered heads because they are the glory of the man, whereas the man is "the image and glory of God." This would seem to imply that the man is in God's image and the woman isn't; but as we have seen, Genesis 1:26–27 makes very clear that both male and female are made in the image of God.

Furthermore, Paul argues that "the woman is of the man," an argument which cannot be substantiated by the Genesis stories of creation. Paul apparently refers to the fact that in Genesis 2, Eve is pictured as created from the rib of Adam; but the first and second chapters of Genesis make clear that God alone is the creator of the human race. When Eve is created, Adam is in a deep sleep. Adam has no more to do with the creation of Eve than he has to do with creating himself.

God is the creator of both Adam and Eve. In I Corinthians 11, Paul seems to remember this and reverse his own argument right in midstream. Having argued for female head-covering because the woman comes from the man, Paul suddenly admits: "In the Lord, however, woman is not independent of man, nor is man independent of woman. But as woman came from man, so also man is born of woman. . . . But everything comes from God" (v. 11 NIV). Even this admission parallels his rabbinic training, however, because the Midrash states, "Neither man without woman, nor woman without man, and neither of them without the divine spirit" (Genesis Rabbah 8:9).[5] Having made that admission, Paul returns to his argument that women should have covered heads when they pray or preach. But he no longer tries to base his argument on the idea that Eve came *from* Adam and was created *for* Adam. Instead he frankly appeals to contemporary customs: "*Judge for yourselves: Is it proper* for a woman to pray to God with her head uncovered? *Does not the very nature of things teach you* that if a man has long hair, it is a disgrace to him, but that if a woman has long hair, it is her glory? For long hair is given to her as a covering. If anyone wants to be contentious about this, *we have no other practice*—nor do the churches of God" (I Corinthians 11:13–16 NIV; emphasis mine).

As our study of socialization showed us, "the very nature of things" will inevitably reflect whatever our culture considers "proper" for women or for men. If we are in a culture where women construct all the houses, then "the very nature of things" will teach us that it is not "proper" for men to construct houses. When we "judge for ourselves," we will inevitably judge according to the standards which our culture holds, standards which have been socialized into us from our earliest childhood. For instance, conservative Christians sometimes assume that men are naturally more creative and have more initiative than women, and impose this view upon the Bible, without realizing that such assumptions are merely the products of our culture's sex-role socialization process.

Surely it is significant that Paul begins by basing female covering on a theological argument for the primacy of the male, then suddenly stops to recognize the primacy of God over both male and female, and then returns to support female covering by a frank appeal to contemporary social customs. With four different phrases—"Judge for yourselves," "Is it proper?" "Does not the nature of things teach you?" and "We have no other practice [custom]"—Paul tries to alert his readers to the fact that he is no longer using a theological underpinning for female covering but has relinquished that in favor of a cultural argument.

It would seem that in this one passage we have a chart of Paul's mind. Trained by one of the best of the Jewish scholars and a product of his culture just as much as we are products of ours, Paul instinctively ("naturally") thinks women should be subordinate. When he reads Genesis 2, he thinks that the story of Adam's rib indicates that Eve is created subordinate to Adam, because that is what tradition teaches about Genesis 2. But there is nothing in the *text* of Genesis 2 which implies subordination, and even tradition admits that women and men are interdependent, both dependent upon the divine spirit. Paul has elsewhere written that in the Christ there is neither male nor female. So his conscience makes him uneasy as he uses the argument of woman-from-man, and he stops to admit that "everything comes from God" and that woman is no more a product of man than man is a product of woman. When he returns to his opinion that women should wear long hair as a covering, he no longer uses the traditional *theology* but switches to an honest and overt appeal to *custom*.

Further indications of Paul's inner conflicts about women also exist within the book of I Corinthians. In chapter 11, as we have seen, Paul has no objections to female praying and prophesying as long as the head is covered. But just three chapters later he is saying that women may not speak at all in church services, "for it is disgraceful for a woman to speak in the church" (14:35 NIV). Again one is reminded of the Megillah's concern for disgracing the *dignity* of the congregation should a woman be permitted to read Torah aloud.

In I Corinthians 15, Paul provides a comprehensive list of all the postresurrection appearances of Jesus but completely omits the first appearance, the appearance to Mary Magdalene (Mark 16:9; John 20:14) or to the women (Matthew 28:9). Why? Since he was trying to give proofs of the resurrection that could not be refuted, he left out the witness of the women. In his heavily patriarchal culture where women could not be legal witnesses, mention of women as witnesses to the resurrection would have weakened rather than strengthened his case. Like us all, Paul was a product of his own culture. He sometimes yielded to his own conditioning or, as is probable in this case, felt forced to accommodate his arguments to the assumptions of his readers.

Again in I Timothy 2:11–15, Paul argues for female subjection on the basis of Genesis 2, the order of creation. There is doubt that the apostle Paul is actually the author of this segment, which may have been interpolated at a later period; but for our purposes such arguments are beside the point, since the book attributes itself to Paul and appears in the canon of Holy Scripture. At any rate, the author argues that woman may neither teach nor usurp authority over man because "Adam was first formed, then Eve."

In other words, the author relies in a *literal* fashion on Genesis 2, the story of Adam's rib, that beautiful embodiment of the parenthood of God and the fact that all human beings are members of one family under God. Are we intended to take Genesis 2 in complete literalness? Are we supposed to regard Genesis 2 as a negation of the statement in Genesis 1 that male and female were created simultaneously and both in the image of God? Are we to insist on the literalness of Adam's being made out of a handful of dust, and that this happened before trees were made to spring up, and before the wild beasts and birds were made, and before Eve? Or are we going to recognize that Genesis 2 is a poetic narrative? It begins and ends with the creation of humanity and sandwiches all God's other creative acts in between, in order to give primacy to the zenith of the creation, the image of God in men and women. Only if we are willing to be literal about every other detail in the narrative can we be literal about the sequence of Adam first, then Eve.

But unless we are willing to place the literal details of Genesis 2 in conflict with the generalization of Genesis 1, we cannot go along with Paul's reasoning process that women must keep silent *because of the order of creation*. If we want to preserve the unity of Genesis, we must interpret the first two chapters in harmony with each other, rather than in conflict—and then we will be up against a serious problem in trying to make the Pauline argument hold water. On the other hand, if we insist on upholding the validity of Paul's reasoning process, we are going to have serious problems making harmony between Genesis 1 and 2. And once Paul's argument is recognized as using Genesis 2 in a literal fashion belied by the poetic nature of the narrative, the theological basis of the argument collapses. We are forced to recognize that the famous sections on women in the church are simply *descriptions* of first-century customs applied to specific situations in local churches.

In Galations 3:28 Paul teaches the equality of Christian men and women: "There is neither Jew nor Greek, there is neither bond nor free, there is neither male nor female: for ye are all one in Christ Jesus." That and similar passages indicate that although Paul's training led him to believe that males are primary in the order of creation, he also believed that the gospel of Christ *revolutionized* that order in significant ways, including the status of women. By insisting on the few Pauline subordination passages and stopping short of the many Pauline liberation passages, Christians have been denying the full impact of the gospel of Christ as it had entered Paul's experience and as it was intended to modify human society.

Further evidence of conflict between Paul's background and his new insights comes in the contrast between I Corinthians 14:34 and Galatians 3:17–19. In the former passage Paul based his argument for female silence on "the law," while in Galatians Paul made clear that the law was a temporary measure, fulfilled and superceded by entrance into the New Creation (Christ). And why did Paul impose silence on women *because of Eve* (I Timothy 2:12–14) when he himself taught that in Christ women as well as men become "new creatures" (II Corinthians 5:17; Galatians 3:29)? The new woman is no longer Eve but Mary; no longer the old humanity (Adam) but the new humanity (Christ). Each of these Pauline contrasts reinforces the impression that according to his training Paul believed in female subordination but that according to his transformed vision he believed that the gospel conferred full equality on all believers.

Many people fear that if they admit that some of Paul's arguments undergirding female submission reflect his training and human limitations, the admission will undercut the authority of Scripture and the doctrine of divine inspiration.

For instance, the theologian who wrote *Man as Male and Female* is repeatedly accused of deserting the evangelical view of Scripture because he says that Paul contradicts himself on the subject of women.[6] Things have come to a bad pass when we have to avoid seeing certain facts of Scripture (or avoid *admitting* that we see them) in order to preserve our preconceived notions about inspiration. Rather, we ought to have so much faith in the God of the Bible that we fearlessly study what is written there.

It does not seem to me detrimental to the authority of Scripture to recognize that some of Paul's arguments *do* reflect his human limitations. C. S. Lewis has pointed out that the imprecatory psalms which express David's vindictive hatred of his enemies are reflections of David's human limitations. For instance, Psalm 109:10 prays that David's enemy's children may all be beggars; Psalm 137:9 pronounces a blessing on anyone who bashes out the brains of an enemy's baby. As Lewis indicates, such hatred violates the spirit of Old Testament instructions like "Rejoice not when thine enemy falleth" (Proverbs 24:17). Yet even the imprecatory psalms were written for our instruction and learning.[7] And I believe that Paul's arguments for female subordination, which contradict much of his own behavior and certain other passages he himself wrote, were also written for our instruction: to show us a basically godly human being in process, struggling with his own socialization; and to force us to use our heads in working our way through conflicting evidence. As if to encourage us to take this view, Paul indicates that he himself is aware of varying levels of inspiration. For instance, in I Corinthians 7:25 he says that concerning virgins he has no command from God and is using his own judgment.

What C. S. Lewis wrote concerning the imprecatory psalms, I would say concerning Paul's rationalization for the female subordination that was standard in his culture: the passages are distorted by the human instrument, yet they are instructive in showing us an honest man in conflict with himself. Lewis calls David's imprecatory psalms "contemptible," yet he insists that we must not try to explain them away, nor must we reject the inspirational and devotional value of the psalms, nor must we try to call hatred a good and pious thing. Rather, we must seek to profit from this record of David's human failings.

Similarly, we cannot deny that Paul rationalized female subordination in a theological fashion that he did not employ concerning slavery. Neither can we deny that Paul rises above these rationalizations in Galatians 3:28, in his many passages on the new creation in Christ, in his instructions concerning mutual submission, and in his own behavior toward female church leaders. We must open our eyes to these conflicts, demonstrating faith in the God who allowed them to appear in the New Testament. We must conquer our fear that honest attention to what we see in the Bible will undercut the doctrine of inspiration. We must allow the facts of Scripture to teach us in what way it is inspired, rather than forcing Scripture to conform to our own theories about it.

Let us, then, courageously recognize that Paul's human limitations do crop up in his arguments undergirding female subordination, believing that these inner conflicts were recorded for our instruction in righteousness by the inspiration of God. As Dr. Calvin J. Roetzel comments: "It would be remarkable indeed if Paul did not reflect some of the prejudice, superstition, and bias of his own time. . . . It seems unfair to denounce him for not anticipating and addressing concerns that have only recently been raised to a high level of consciousness. . . . It is the gospel which Paul preaches rather than his limited application and witness to it that is definitive for our time "[8] Despite traditional theories that Genesis 2 depicts the order of creation and that female submission is based on that order, Paul treated Phoebe and Priscilla and other women as his equals in God's work; and it is time for the Christian community to follow Paul in his transcendence of his limitations instead of clinging to the letter of his struggles with them.

The Bible was not in error to record David's hatred, and the Bible was not in error to record Paul's thought-processes. But *we* are in error to absolutize anything that denies the thrust of the entire Bible toward individual wholeness and harmonious community, toward oneness in the New Creation.

6
Learning to
Interpret Accurately

Even if the biblical evidence were 50 percent in support of female subordination and only 50 percent in favor of the equality of mutual submission, ordinary kindness and decency should lead modern Christians to choose in favor of equality. But the evidence for Christian equality is far stronger than that.

The word *evidence* leads us into consideration of the two problems which most often worry Bible believers when they are confronted with indications that Paul's human limitations show up in his writings and that we cannot continue absolutizing the biblical culture where women are concerned. The first problem focuses on biblical evidence in general: Can the Bible be used to prove just anything the arguer wants to prove? The second problem is closely related to the first: if we concede that the Bible does teach male-female equality in the home and in the church, then we are admitting that it has been misinterpreted for centuries. Where will the process of reinterpreting the Bible stop, once we make such an admission? Will we be forced into total relativism? Will we lose all sense of absolutes? Will we, by granting male-female equality, in effect be destroying the authority of the Bible over our lives?

First things first. Yes, the Bible can be used to prove almost anything—to the prover's own satisfaction, that is. We all know the story of the person who "proved" that the Bible advises suicide by pointing to two proof-texts: Matthew 27:3, which says that Judas hanged himself; and Luke 10:37, which says "Go and do likewise." But, of course, such "proof," with no attention to context or logical connectives, would never be called proof by any disinterested and serious student.

As a matter of fact, it is simply not true that any theory in the world can be supported from the Bible—not if we are talking about honest, open, careful interpretation. Civilization has grown more and more subjective and relativistic. As a result, the teacher of literature must work harder and harder to convince students that, no, a piece of literature *cannot* mean just anything the reader wants it to mean. Instead, the reader must learn to pay attention to the author's choice of words, rhythms, sentence structures, images or word pictures, point of view, and so forth, in order to experience what the work actually embodies. Simply to breeze through poems or novels, investing them with whatever the reader is inclined to think the work ought to be saying, is not to read but to daydream and indulge in projection. Good reading involves discipline. Although there may always be disagreement between the interpretations arrived at by well-trained readers, the differences will usually be ones of emphasis and application rather than of fact.

And if secular literature requires self-discipline and training, how much more does the Bible require and deserve well-trained, carefully disciplined readers! The more one believes that the Bible is divinely inspired, the more eager one should be to read with precision and alert attention to detail. Yet many people who have read the Bible through literally *dozens* of times have never noticed that the story of creation in Genesis 2 has a different plot from the story in Genesis 1! I am aware of that because I was one such reader for many years. Even after I had completed my Ph.D. in English literature, having read the book of Genesis perhaps fifty times, I had never noticed the plot differences between the two stories of creation until I looked specifically to try to disprove the claim of a feminist author that the accounts differed from each other. Although I could readily discern the most minute differences in other literary accounts, I had been so thoroughly taught that there could be no contradictions or errors in the inspired Bible that I blocked myself from the alert reading I gave to less important texts. And by refusing to see the surface facts of Scripture, I, of course, also blocked off the profound realizations that come only after pondering the meaning of discrepancies like those which exist between Genesis 1 and 2. I can no longer risk the loss of such growth.

In order to learn all that we possibly can, then, we must approach the Bible prayerfully but also with all our rational faculties alert and aware. And at the same time we must obey various principles of good reading which will keep us from the wild excesses of our friend who felt that the Bible advocated suicide. One of the principles of good reading is that before we do anything else we must try to grasp the literal meaning of a passage as it was probably understood at the time of its first writing. For this purpose, we must study the meanings of the words used, their grammatical connectives, and their historical backgrounds. If we do not know Hebrew and Greek, we must make use of analytical concordances which clarify for us which word is being used and where else it has been used, interlinear translations which clarify the grammatical structures for us, and scholarly commentaries which help to bring us closer to the original literal meaning of the author.

We must pay attention to the point of view in the passage, asking ourselves questions like these: Who was the author? Where was he living and under what conditions? To whom was this author writing? What was the occasion? What is the tone or emotional attitude of the author?

When we are reading dialogue, it is important to ask ourselves such questions as these: What is the tone of the various individual speakers? Are they angry with one another, or are they on good terms? Is one trying to trap the other? If so, is the answer given affected by the attitude of the questioner? For instance, people repeatedly asked Jesus questions, not because they wanted to learn but because they wanted to catch him in error. As we read his answers, we have to allow for the possibility that his irritation with their motives has led him to be as absolute or crushing as possible. This would not cause us to *discount* his sayings, of course, but to respond more adequately to their tone.

No matter what passage we are reading, it is important to ask ourselves about the literary form in which the ideas are cast. Is the passage written as straightforward exposition, intended to explain a concept, as in Romans 12:1–2, or to describe an actual event, as in Acts 2:14–36? Or is the passage making use of literary forms such as poetry (Acts 2:25–28, where Peter quotes a psalm of David) or parable (Luke 15)? If the form is literary, what accommodations must be made because of the literary structure? For instance, the parable form in Luke 15 should alert us to the fact that these stories are not literally about sheep, coins, and children but about God's caring for the salvation of the lost (vv. 7, 10, 32). At the same time, the nature of the parable as an illustration of religious principles alerts us to the importance of the fact that Jesus has used three leading characters to represent God—a shepherd, a householder, and a "certain man" who had two sons—and that the householder was a *woman*. Although the central point of these parables is not to teach us that God is unlimited by human sexual polarities of male or female, one of the *side effects* of Jesus' choice of characters is to make exactly that point.

We must also ask ourselves whether any unfamiliar idioms are being used—that is, whether some of the expressions might have been familiar to the time and place of the first writing but are unfamiliar to us. We especially have to beware of word usage which *seems* familiar but in which the word's meaning in the modern world is drastically different from its meaning at the time the Bible was written. For instance, in I Corinthians 11:3, Paul says that "the head of every man is Christ, and the head of the woman is the man, and the head of Christ is God" (NIV). We, of course, assume that we know very well the meaning of "*head*." Anybody knows that the head makes the decisions for the body, so the passage has been interpreted to mean that the Christ makes the decisions for man, man makes the decisions for woman, and God makes the decisions for the Christ. But in biblical times, it was not known that the head makes the decisions and gives the orders to the nervous system. Decision-making was located in the *heart*, which is why we are told that our belief in Jesus is to take place in our hearts and that thoughts issue from the heart (Romans 10:9; Matthew 15:19; Hebrews 4:12; and so forth). So the passage cannot be a discussion of the head as the decision-maker.

We are then forced to study the context in order to understand the meaning of "headship" here; and the context makes clear that Paul is speaking of the head as the source or origin, as we speak of the head of a stream. In this passage, Paul uses the traditional interpretation of Genesis 2 in order to argue that woman must cover her head when she prays or prophesies, because man is her source of origin (vv. 8–9). As we have seen, he soon abandons this argument in an honest recognition that, in reality, God is the source (head) of both male and female. But the confusion over the meaning of *head* is a good example of the confusion which results when we heedlessly "read in" modern meanings for ancient word usages.

Above all, we must place the passage in context. The context of a passage includes the flow of thought that immediately precedes and follows the passage in question; and here it is important to remember that the chapter and verse divisions were added by editors for convenience and are not to be confused with divinely inspired sectionings. Beyond the flow of the individual passage, the context is the whole book in which the passage appears. If we find ourselves saying that a certain verse has a meaning that runs counter to the overall meaning of the biblical book in which it occurs, we must admit to ourselves that there is something wrong with our interpretation.

And beyond the individual book, there is the context of the whole Bible, where the same principle holds true. Our suicidal friend would have known that his two proof-texts do not add up to advice about committing suicide had he paid any attention to the life-affirming thrust of the whole Bible. When attempting to place a given passage in the context of the whole Bible, it is also important to remember another principle: the Bible uses the language of accommodation concerning God and the universe so that God is said to have eyes and hands and so forth, and the earth is said to have four corners.

Only after the literal meaning is firmly established is it acceptable to move toward secondary levels of meaning. Any symbolic, spiritual, mystical, figurative, or allegorical meanings must depend upon and be harmonized with the literal level of meaning. Otherwise, indeed, any passage could be twisted to mean anything the reader wants it to mean. For instance, suppose someone wanted to get rid of the egalitarian message of Galatians 3:28 by saying that the passage refers to some far future time, some future dispensation when God will completely do away with our bodies so that there will be no Jew or Greek, no slave or free person, and no male or female. This interpretation can be shown to be false by several means.

First, by placing Galatians 3:28 in the context of the whole Bible we remember that the Bible teaches the *resurrection* of the body, not the *destruction* of the body. What is buried a natural body will be raised a spiritual body (I Corinthians 15:44). Therefore, Galatians 3:28 cannot mean that at some future time we will be completely removed from our bodies.

Furthermore, the Bible teaches that Christians are to be *currently* engaged in growing more Christlike (Ephesians 4:11–16 and so forth). So to postpone spiritual union in the body of Christ until some future dispensation would be to ignore the Bible's continual emphasis on present-tense loving-kindness and unity.

Second, by paying attention to the literal level of the argument concerning Jews and Greeks, we can draw some pretty clear conclusions about the sexual meaning of the verse. The major flow of argument surrounding Galatians 3:28 concerns whether the Christians newly converted from paganism (the Greeks) should have to conform to Jewish religious customs and laws. Paul argues that, no, they need not conform to Jewish customs, because by becoming children of the Christ they have automatically achieved full status as the children of Abraham and need not earn it (v. 29).

Since everyone who has been baptized into Christ has "put on Christ" (like a new outfit of clothes), there is now to be no artificial barrier between Jew and Greek, slave and free, male and female. Paul clearly could not mean that by turning Christian, the Jews and Greeks would instantly lose their ethnic roots. The whole context of the argument between Peter and Paul at Antioch (Galatians 2:11–21) makes evident that far from forgetting their ethnicity, the converts were squabbling about their ethnic identity. Paul apparently means that Jewish religious patterns need not be required of the Greek converts. And in a parallel interpretation encouraged by the parallelism of the grammar, Paul is not saying that converts to Christianity lost their biological distinctives as male and female but rather that the dominance and submission behavior patterns which create barriers to male-female fellowship were to be dissolved in the love of Christ.

Third, we can tell that the passage does not refer to the dim, distant future by paying attention to the tenses of the verbs. Verse 27 speaks in the past tense. It has *already hap-*

pened that "all of you who were united with Christ in baptism have been clothed with Christ" (3:27 NIV). And because of what has already happened, something else is *currently* true: within the mystical body of the Christ, there *is* (present tense) oneness of Jew and Greek, slave and free, male and female. The passage, therefore, implies that it is up to the readers to behave in such a way as to make this mystical fact a living reality.

Notice that in this interpretation, the literal meaning of the passage is given primacy. The verb tenses and the context will not allow us to spiritualize Galatians 3:28 by placing its fulfillment in some dim, distant future time. But we come to a point when remaining literal would force us into the absurdity of saying that Paul meant all Christian converts would instantly become unisexual and uniracial. At that point, and only at that point, are we ready to accept a mystical meaning, that Paul is talking about the mystical body of the New Humanity. Even then, the mystical meaning is controlled by the necessity of harmonizing with the thrust of the rest of the passage, the entire book of Galatians, and the whole Bible. No meaning which conflicted with the clear message of any of these could be taken seriously.

Other principles which must operate in our interpretation of the Bible are that the grounds for the interpretation should be made explicit. We should admit when we are guessing or constructing a hypothesis and when we have definite and conclusive support from word studies (lexical proof), Hebrew and Greek studies (grammatical proof), cultural studies (background proof, such as corroboration from contemporary rabbinical writings), or theological studies (proof drawn from the theological systems of Calvin or Luther or some other theologian). And we should usually give preference to the clearest and simplest possible interpretation. For instance, the same Hebrew word means both *side* and *rib;* so in Genesis 2 we can take our choice between Adam's *rib* or Adam's *side* as the raw material God used for the creation of Eve. The choice of *side* tends to involve the reader in the theory that Adam was created hermaphroditic in Genesis 1 and divided into male and female in Genesis 2, while the choice of *rib* seems to be simpler. But either would be acceptable.

Of course, no matter how careful our scholarship, we can never claim to have achieved infallibility. In this connection a rather long quotation from Dr. Bernard Ramm merits our careful attention:

> How do we settle the truth when two people of equal piety and devotion have different opinions? Does the Holy Spirit tell one person the rapture is pre-tribulation, and another that it is post-tribulation? The very fact that spiritually minded interpreters come to different conclusions about these matters distresses many people's minds. They have presumed that if a [person] is yielded to the Holy Spirit his [or her] interpretations must be correct. But certain things must be kept in mind. First, the Holy Spirit gives *nobody* infallible interpretations. Second, piety is a help to interpretation but it is not a substitute for knowledge or study or intelligence. Third, all of us are still in the human body and subject to its limitations and frailties and we make mistakes of interpretation in Scripture as well as errors of judgment in the affairs of life. It is the present temptation of at least American evangelicalism to substitute a class of devout Bible teachers for the Catholic Pope. To such people the *meaning* of Scripture is that which their favorite Bible teacher teaches. But the Protestant principle must always be this: *the truest interpretations are those with the best justification.*[1]

Although none of us can claim infallibility, all of us can try to be precise. We can discipline ourselves not to believe everything we hear and to check all interpretations by questions about context, word usage, grammatical structure, and so forth. We can seek to ground our interpretations in facts.

Facts provide the control over interpretations in the same way that experiments exercise control over scientific hypotheses. If experiments fail to support a scientist's hypothesis, he or she may not simply keep the experiments secret in order to cling to the hypothesis. Anyone who did that would not be respected for long by the scientific community! And if the facts fail to support our interpretations, we cannot shrug off the facts and cling to our interpretations. We must give up any interpretation which runs counter to the facts *within* and *surrounding* Scripture.

Therefore, we see that it is simply not true that the Bible will provide support for just any theory or system devised by the human mind. When interpretations are governed by careful reading method, it is possible to achieve a great deal of clarity, especially on subjects that the Bible treats as frequently as it treats human relationships between male and female. Dr. Ramm's illustration of the exact chronology of the rapture and tribulation is a good example of one of the more obscure matters which divide biblical scholars; but human relating in the Christ-nature is not equally obscure. Careful attention to the facts of first-century culture combined with attention to the thrust of the whole Bible toward human unity in the New Creation will go far toward correcting many of our false conclusions.

Which brings us to the second problem. Many are willing to admit that the Bible teaches male-female equality only if they can be assured that the admission will not open the floodgates of relativism by destroying the authority of the Bible over our lives. I have treated this problem last because I think our discussion of the first problem provides the best answer to the second. In a world of rapid change, we cannot be sure *what* moral or ethical problems we will face in the future. But we can be sure of this: whatever the problems may be, we will get more accurate guidance from the Bible by studying it in depth and by reporting precisely on what we see than by allowing ourselves to see only what we already assume is supposed to be there.

If we construct our own theory of the inspiration of the Bible and assume that what we have been taught is the only way the Bible may ever be read, and if we refuse to listen to any facts to the contrary, then we have substituted our own ideas *about* the Word of God for the Word of God itself. We are no better than the dishonest scientist who falsifies his research to support a theory in which he has invested a great deal of time and energy. And we are no better than the seventeenth-century theologians who refused to look through Galileo's telescope because they were protecting their interpretation of the Bible.

The real way to show respect for the inspiration and authority of the Bible is to trust the Bible to teach us in what way it is inspired. The experience of many serious students of the Bible has taught us that the Bible sometimes records the human limitations of the human beings who were the channels of God's Word to us. How then will we be able to sift out which passages reflect human limitations and which passages reflect the will of God for all times and all places? There is no easy formula. We can do it only by careful study of the text, paying attention to all the methods of precise scholarly interpretation. And we must immediately suspect any reading which contradicts the thrust of the whole Bible toward human justice and oneness in the New Creation.

In this task we may find guidance in Christ's own behavior as recorded in Matthew 19:3–9. When religious leaders tried to trap Jesus by pitting his view of divorce against Mosaic law, Jesus pointed out that Mosaic law did not represent God's original intention for men and women. Rather, the law given in Deuteronomy 24:1–3 was permitted to a patriarchal culture "because your hearts were hard. But it was not this way from the beginning" (NIV). Thus by his own practice Jesus showed us that sacred Scripture concerning man's behavior toward woman does not always reflect God's highest intentions for the human race. Sometimes it reflects cultural conditions which gradually should be regenerated through the power of the gospel.

Jesus himself harks back to God's original intention, when the Creator "made them male and female," as the basis for a single moral standard for men and women. By playing off Deuteronomy against Genesis, Jesus is not questioning the inspiration of the Old Testament but is showing that certain passages were inspired to meet specific needs in response to human hardness, while other passages (recognizable by context) convey God's ultimate intentions for the human race. Unfortunately, for centuries most organized Christian churches have been reversing Jesus' methods where women are concerned, stressing the few repressive passages that address themselves to specific historical situations or attitudes, and ignoring the pervasive and liberating theology of human unity in the spirit of God. It is high time to follow Jesus' example in the interpretation of Scripture.

7
Bible Doctrines
and Human Equality

In the *Post-American* (May, 1975), traditionalist Thomas Howard writes that trying to defend female equality by listing Sarah, Deborah, Esther, Jael, Anna, Dorcas, and Paul's female assistants in the ministry is "self-defeating, since . . . [the list] is embarrassing in its brevity next to the long list of the . . . *male* prophets, apostles, etc." But the point being made by biblical feminists is not that the female list exceeds or equals the male. Rather, in the Bible's patriarchal context, it is amazing and indicative of God's intentions that any women are mentioned at all. Jesus repeatedly had to correct the sexist and stereotyped responses of his male disciples, who were shocked that he would talk to a Samaritan woman and disturbed that mere children should bother the Rabbi and incensed that the Sovereign would let himself be touched by a "fallen woman". What biblical feminists see operating in the Bible is the power of God moving in human beings, causing them to overcome the prejudice of their culture in order to include occasional details about women in leadership roles. It is not the small amount of attention to women which is surprising, but rather that there is as much biblical focus on women as actually exists. And biblical feminists emphasize these passages about women for four reasons: because the church has *not* emphasized them, because Christian women need to be encouraged to believe that they too can be mean-

ingful in God's service, because Christian men need to discover the comfort and joy of working in equal male-female
partnership, and because the sin of sexism must be exorcized
from the modern Christian community.

But Dr. Howard is surely right in the sense that biblical
feminism should not seek to root itself exclusively in the
citation of first-century practices. Despite the purifying impact of the gospel, those practices remain to some degree
patriarchal and sexist. Biblical feminism must instead root
itself firmly in the major Bible *doctrines* of the Trinity, of
creation in the image of God, of the incarnation, and of
regeneration (including the regenerative influence of the gospel in human society.)

We have already dealt with male-female creation in God's
image. And we have explored the implications of the male-
female imagery surrounding the Three Persons of the Trinity,
including the implications for our contemporary theological
language. That leaves us with two major doctrines yet to
explore in connection with male-female relating: the doctrine
of the incarnation, and the doctrine of regeneration.

Actually we have already touched upon the doctrine of the
incarnation by saying that Christ's human nature was referred
to by New Testament authors not as *anēr*, male, but as *anthrōpos*, human. The implication, of course, is that the Christ
became a human being, a person, rather than first and fore-
most a male. Jesus came into the world, not only as the Savior
of the world, but to provide the image of spiritual perfection,
of full physical and mental health, of the human ideal. Emphasis on his maleness would have tended to exclude women
from participation in this human ideal. This may well be the
reason the New Testament authors never mention any marriage, although they do mention Jesus' warm personal relationships with women as well as men. Those relationships,
and Jesus' refusal to participate in the taboos that de-
humanized women, point toward the probability that one of

Jesus' missions in the world was to bring healing for the dominance-submission, one-up, one-down pattern of male-female relating.

At this point, however, it might be helpful to focus on two aspects of the incarnation which seem to have been widely misunderstood and misused in connection with the controversy over women's liberation. On the one hand, some secular feminists have heaped scorn on the concept of Christ's submissive suffering, blaming the whole concept for the oppression of women. "You have taught women to accept suffering in a Christlike fashion," they have argued, "and have turned them into martyrs. It isn't healthy." On the other hand, traditionalists have praised the submission of Christ to the will of the First Person, making it the model that Christian women should follow in relations with their husbands. "Jesus *voluntarily* submitted himself to the will of God," they say, "and that is the model for all healthy Christian women. They should voluntarily submit themselves to male headship in order to find true liberation. Just as Christ's submission to the Father did not imply any inferiority, the Christian woman's subordination in home and church does not imply inferiority to the male—only a different role."

Since the earthly subordination of Jesus to the will of the First Person is a matter of importance to both traditionalists and feminists, it is worth examining at some length. According to Philippians 2:5–8, "The divine nature was [Christ's] from the first; yet [the Christ] did not think to snatch at equality with God, but *made* [self] nothing, assuming the nature of a slave. Bearing the human likeness, revealed in human shape, [the Christ] *humbled* [self], and in obedience accepted even death—death on a cross" (NIV; emphasis mine). What we see here is a divine being who voluntarily chose, for a *specific purpose*, to be emptied of the divine nature in order to become human (note: not primarily *male*, but *human*) and even to become the *dregs* of humanity by dying a slave's death, crucifixion.

Jesus' submission to the will of the First Person while on earth is here pictured as a model to demonstrate how all human beings ought to relate to the divine Being. Once the Christ had become human, Jesus obeyed the divine will. Traditionalists who try to make this the model for male-female relationships overlook the important fact that the Christ first possessed the divine nature, voluntarily laid its prerogatives aside to become human, and for the duration of life on earth showed *all* of us how *each* human being ought to relate to God.

To use the anology that the wife is to the husband as Christ-on-earth is to the Father is to make the male the equivalent of the First Person of the Trinity—and then we are back into the idolatry of the masculine that was discussed in chapter 2. Interestingly enough, the Bible really *does* use the model of Christ's self-humbling in the context of marital relationships, in Ephesians 5. But there Jesus' voluntary self-humiliation is pictured as a model for the Christian *husband,* not for the wife at all! It would seem that the traditionalists who urge women to emulate Jesus' humble obedience to the Father have gotten things rather confused. Biblically speaking, Jesus' life as a human being submissive to the First Person in order to redeem humanity is the model for the Christian husband to follow, loving his wife "just as Christ loved the church and gave [self] up for her." And the model for wives is the model of the church's submission in response to the self-sacrifice of Christ—a profound mystery, as Paul admits (Ephesians 5:32). According to this model, the Christian husband must *lead the way* in self-giving concern and deference toward his wife, to which the Christian wife in return responds with respect and deference.

Had the Bible used the model of the Christ's submission to

the First Person as the model of woman's submission to her husband, we would have been faced with a clear model of the male as divine (therefore dominant) and the female as human (therefore submissive). Instead the model is that of the Christ *in human form* giving up self for the church, and the church's submission in response to that self-sacrificial love. So instead of a dominance and submission model, we have a mutual submission model. According to this model or metaphor, the incarnation of the Christ for the purpose of dying to redeem the church represents the giving up of the self-will of the Christian husband in relation to his wife. The voluntary submission of the wife comes about in response to the *prior* voluntary submission of the husband, since there could be no church until the Christ had *first* died to redeem the church. No wonder the whole metaphor is presented to us in the context of *mutual* submission: "Submit to one another out of reverence for Christ" (Ephesians 5:21 NIV).

Those who are disturbed that the husband is compared to Christ while the wife is compared only to the human church are, I think, forgetting that the analogy is not to Christ-as-divine but to Christ-as-self-emptied, Christ-as-flesh, Christ-giving-self-up. Unlike the extrabiblical metaphor of wifely submission as the Christ submitted to the First Person, this metaphor does not picture woman as human and man as divine. The emphasis is on the human nature of Christ, the self-sacrifice of Christ, which in turn calls forth submission from the church. "We love because [Christ] first loved us" (I John 4:19).

Admittedly, the analogy between husband and Christ-as-self-giving breaks down when Paul speaks of Christ as the Savior (Ephesians 5:23), since husbands are in no sense the Saviors of their wives—unless Paul meant that by self-sacrificial love, Christian husbands would be saving their wives from patriarchal oppression. But Paul believed, with the rabbis, that the husband is the source (head) of the wife as Christ is the source (head) of the church; and Jesus was the source of the church precisely because of being its Savior. As the whole church is subject to the Christ (who is the nature shared by everyone), wives are to be subject to their husbands and husbands are to love their wives, both of them submitting to each other out of reverence for the Christ, the whole church (Ephesians 5:21).

It is also important to notice that Jesus' obedience is not to some totally external power. Repeatedly Jesus stresses the fact of *oneness* with God (John 10:30; John 17:11; and so forth). So when Philippians talks about the Christ's obedience, the obedience is not to something or someone external. We are told that the Christ made *self* into nothing, humbled *self*. So Jesus' obedience is to a will-power and determination which was *within* himself but which also reached far beyond his own private interests. He was willing to give up his life for a goal which was more important than his own private fate. In other words, his individual will was fused with a universal divine will. He and God were one.

This is an important point because for years women have been socialized to give up their will by catering to the will of their fathers or husbands. In an *ideal* male-female Christian relationship, this would work out beautifully because the father or husband would already be following the example of the Christ in a self-giving concern for the women in his life. But for years Christians have been following a patriarchal dominance-submission pattern. And human nature, alas, does not tend toward self-sacrifice when given absolute power. So the practical result has been that women have been forced, through the power of socialization, to give up their will to a will which is external to them and frequently unconcerned about them. Some women have been crushed under such a system. Others have fought back and become vicious and cruel. Still others have learned to be subtly undercutting and slyly manipulative.

But there is hope! In a male-female relationship of mutual submission under God, it should be possible to achieve something very similar to Jesus' obedience to the First Person and simultaneously to himself: a oneness, an interconnection of interests, a mutual concern that goes beyond the merely selfish interests of either partner to include the best interests of both partners in particular, and of the human race in general.

In this connection, the Virgin Mary is often pictured as the female principle submitting to an external male principle. The visit of the angel Gabriel and the coming of the Holy Spirit upon her are interpreted as intrusions of the masculine power of God. To this masculine power her feminine, submissive nature replies, "Be it unto me according to thy word." And then, of course, Mary is held up as an example to Christian women of how they ought to relate to their husbands and their pastors (who of course should be male!). But here again, as in the case of Jesus' submission to the will of the First Person, closer examination will not bear out such an interpretation.

The first chapter of Luke reveals not one but *two* visits of Gabriel to human beings for the purpose of announcing a supernatural birth. First, Gabriel visits Zechariah in the temple to tell him that despite the fact that he and Elizabeth were childless and were now too old to have children, Elizabeth would bear a son, to be called John, who would be a great man of God. Then six months later Gabriel visits Mary to tell her that she will have a son by the power of the Holy Ghost. Both of these births, according to Gabriel, are proof that "nothing is impossible with God" (Luke 1:37).

The rest of us may never experience literal visits from archangels or the kind of supernatural births granted to Elizabeth and Mary. But we do have moments when we feel the Holy Spirit's presence upon us and the overshadowing power of the Most High (Luke 1:35). For instance, we may be writing a letter to someone in need, and suddenly we find ourselves expressing ideas better than we ever have before, even saying things we did not know we knew, because of a surge of strength inside us which we recognize as a helping power from beyond ourselves. Or someone hurts us, and in response we feel an understanding and forgiveness which astonishes us because we know it is not "in us" to be so patient—again, we can sense something operating in us which is a power beyond ourselves. So in the terms of our everyday human experience, the visit of the angel, the creative overshadowing of Mary by the power of the Highest, and the coming of the Holy Spirit upon her are all symbols of God's internal workings within our human personalities.

In other words, God is not exclusively *out there;* God is *in here* also, inside us, working within and through our own personalities. God is not an *external* force, let alone a *masculine* force. God is Person, the Spirit or Ground or Structure or Process of everything which is real in the entire universe, indwelling everything which has been made and yet not limited by what has been made. What Mary's submission pictures is not the feminine principle submitting to the masculine principle, but the fusion of the individual private will to a will which stretches far beyond private interests. She yielded to a divine will which existed *within* herself as well as *beyond* herself.

Many Christians have made a serious error by picturing God too exclusively in transcendent terms, as if God were completely removed from humanity and the natural world. We have feared pantheism, which involves denial of God's personhood by equating God with the forces and laws of the universe. Pantheists assume that God is totally immanent, completely contained within that which is created and therefore limited by it. Because we have shied away from pantheism, we have gone to the opposite extreme and spoken as if God were completely transcendent, completely above and beyond and outside of the created universe (including ourselves). Many of us have forgotten or under-emphasized the fact that God is both *outside* and *within* the creation, immanent as well as transcendent, indwelling what has been made and yet not limited to what has been made (Acts 17:24–28; Luke 17:20–21). We tend to forget the clear depiction of God as both transcendent and immanent in such passages as Ephesians 4:6, which speaks of "one God and Father of all, who is *over* all and *through* all and *in* all" (NIV; emphasis mine). So Mary's submission is not to an external force, nor to a masculine force, but to a divine will which existed within herself as well as external to herself. By giving her energies to an internal power which extended far beyond her own private interests, she was being true to the law of her own personality.

It makes a big difference to a person's self-concept to realize that submission to God does not mean surrender to something completely external to the self, but rather fusion of the private will with a universal concern that goes beyond selfish private interest. When we submit to God, we willingly harmonize our internal willpower to the will of an almighty God who is "over all and through all and in all." The mutual submission and mutual serving of all Christians is an expression of this kind of harmonization. "God is love. Whoever lives in love *lives in God,* and *God in* [*them*]." (I John 4:16*b* NIV; emphasis mine).

It is interesting to compare the reactions of Zechariah and Mary to the announcement of Gabriel. Told that he and his barren wife will have a son in their old age, Zechariah doubts the word of God: "How can I be sure of this?" (Luke 1:18 NIV). Told that she, a virgin, will bear a son, Mary asks only the *method* of its happening but expresses no doubt that it will indeed happen: "'How can this be,' Mary asked the angel, 'since I am a virgin?'" (Luke 1:34 NIV). Although he was a very righteous man, Zechariah did not fully sense the power of God within his own being, so he wanted some sort of proof that what the angel told him was really true. As a result, Gabriel told him that he would be unable to speak until his son was born, "Because you did not believe my words, which will come true at their proper time" (Luke 1:20 NIV). On the other hand, Mary was fully in tune with the God who is "over all and through all and in all." Because she lived in love, God lived in her and she in God. After the miraculous conception, she sings that "the Mighty One has done great things for me. . . . [God] has filled the hungry with good things. . . . [God] has helped [God's] servant Israel" (Luke 1:49, 53, 54 NIV). These are remarkable images of *God as servant to human beings*, who in response serve God. When all the images are considered carefully, the story of the incarnation presents a beautiful picture of mutual service, a fusing of human willpower with the power of God.

Conversely, when men and women are taught that the feminine principle is passivity and the masculine principle is activity, each half of the human race is cut off from full human personhood. Full humanity requires sometimes activity, sometimes passivity, in a fluid and unstereotyped interchange. And when men and women are taught that God is totally external to themselves, both halves of the human race are divorced from the joyful realization that God is not only "over all" but also "through all" and "in all." That *all* includes me. That *all* includes you. Miraculously, joyously, by living in love, by living in mutual service and mutual submission, males and females alike can live in God and experience God's living in us! Spiritually speaking, males can carry Christ within their bodies just as surely as Mary carried Christ in her womb. And females can rejoice with Zechariah that God keeps God's word and enables us "to serve [God] without fear in holiness and righteousness before [God] all our days" (Luke 1:74–75 NIV).

Finally, the equality of male and female is grounded in the doctrine of the New Creation in the Christ-nature. According to Christian doctrine, the Bible shows us the natural universe (creation) in three stages: a "very good" stage, fresh from the hands of the Creator (Genesis 1 and 2); a fallen, corrupted, suffering stage (Genesis 3 and following); and a stage of future perfection, already begun in those who have become the children of God, but not to be completed until after Christ's return. Romans 8:18–24 (NEB) gives us a clear concept of the present and future stages of the creation:

> For I reckon that the sufferings we now endure bear no comparison with the splendour, as yet unrevealed, which is in store for us. For the created universe waits with eager expectation for God's [children] to be revealed. It was made the victim of frustration . . . yet always there was hope, because the universe itself is to be freed from the shackles of mortality and enter upon the liberty and splendour of the children of God. Up to the present, we know, the whole created universe groans in all its parts as if in the pangs of childbirth. Not only so, but even we, to whom the Spirit is given as firstfruits of the harvest to come, are groaning inwardly while we wait for God to make us [God's children] and set our whole body free.

People of faith living in a fallen world are therefore hampered by many limitations, but we already have the Spirit within us as the promise of the glory that is to follow. We are *already* part of the New Creation which is to be perfected in the future. Therefore, Paul is able to write in Colossians 3:9–11 (NIV): "you have taken off your old self with its practices and have put on the new self, which is being renewed in knowledge in the image of its Creator. Here there is no Greek or Jew, circumcised or uncircumcised, barbarian, Scythian, slave or free, but Christ is all, and is in all." Because we are new selves in a new creation, under process of renewal in the image of our Creator, we are intended to relate to one another without prejudice and without artificial human barriers or mind-forged manacles.

As we have seen, there is no hint of dominance and submission in the relationship of Adam and Eve before the fall into sin. Genesis 1:28 says that God gave to both male and female a joint commission to subdue the earth and rule over every living thing. Genesis 2:23–24 uses a pun on the Hebrew words for *man* and *woman* to emphasize the oneness of the human race: "This shall be called woman (*ishshah*) for from man (*ish*) was this taken. That is why a man leaves his father and mother and is united to his wife, and the two become one flesh."

The first time dominance and submission enter into the male-female relationship is after the fall. Genesis 3:14–19 pronounces a curse on the serpent and a curse on the ground, because of sin. God does not *curse* Adam and Eve, but he does *describe* to them the unpleasant changes that have been brought about because of their alienation from the Ground of their own Being (God). For one thing, childbearing will become painful. For another, work will become burdensome; people will have to sweat and will feel frustrated by nature's unfriendly thorns and thistles. For another, life will move toward death, toward a return to the accursed ground. And for another, men will exert dominance over their wives. These are not *pre*scriptions. They are simply *de*scriptions of the quality of human life in a fallen world.

Recognizing these matters as descriptions, civilization has done its best to overcome the painful and unpleasant consequences of the fall. We have tried to alleviate the pangs of childbirth. We have invented labor-saving devices to reduce the sweat of mankind and to regain control over nature. We have tried desperately, though unsuccessfully, to overcome death. But interestingly enough, there has been no concerted effort to overcome the tendency of males to dominate females.

There is no shocked outcry from the Christian world when Christian husbands act domineering or Christian wives act manipulative. For instance, *Redbook* magazine presents an interview with Marabel Morgan and her husband which explains what motivated her to write her best seller, *The Total*

Woman. Mrs. Morgan had made some family plans for a certain evening. But just the evening before those plans were to be carried out, her husband casually mentioned that they'd be spending the next evening with some of his business associates. When Mrs. Morgan protested, Mr. Morgan said in an icy voice, "From now on, when I plan for us to go somewhere, I will tell you twenty minutes ahead of time. You'll have time to get ready, and we'll do all this without arguing." Mrs. Morgan ran upstairs and wept and then did as she was told; in an attempt to adjust to her husband's mastery over her, she wrote her book, which supplies advice concerning how women can *manipulate* their husbands and masters into giving them what they want.

The Morgans summarize their own marriage this way: he says, "We try a lot," and she says, "I cry a lot."[1] Mr. Morgan calls women's liberation "organized selfishness" but does not seem to catch even a glimpse of his own self-centeredness. Although the Morgans claim that theirs is a Christian and biblical marriage, Mr. Morgan sees no need to obey Paul's directive to "submit to one another out of reverence for Christ" (Ephesians 5:21 NIV). Submission is only for women! And Mrs. Morgan seems unaware of her Christian responsibility to "in all things grow up into [Christ]" (Ephesians 4:15). Yet *The Total Woman* has been taught as an adult-education course in hundreds of Christian churches all over the country!

Why have such attitudes been supported rather than repudiated by Christian clergy and Christian churches? Part of the problem lies in assuming that Genesis 3:16 prescribes God's ideal for the human race rather than simply describing the sinful results of the fall of humanity. To be consistent, however, anybody who advocates wifely submission and male domination on that basis should also refuse to use pain-alleviating drugs and techniques, should get rid of all labor-

saving devices, and should earn food by sweating in the fields
without any power tools.

It is ridiculous enough for the secular world to uphold male
domination while seeking relief from all the other sad results
of the fall. But for *Christians* to support male domination is
the height of folly! The Bible teaches that "when anyone is
united to Christ, there is a new world; the old order has gone,
and a new order has already begun" (II Corinthians 5:17
NEB). Even if Genesis 3 *had* been meant as a prescription of
what fallen civilization of necessity had to be like, it is clear
that uniting with the Christ-nature is supposed to move us out
of the old order into a completely new order. In this new
order, there is no discrimination based upon differences of
race, economic status, or sex (Colossians 3:11; Galatians 3:28).
The male barking of orders to a weeping but submissive
female is patriarchal. It is the sinful condition described in
Genesis 3:16. It is absolutely opposed to the Christian way of
relating. As the apostle Paul puts it: "You, my friends, were
called to be free [persons]; only do not turn your freedom into
licence for your lower nature, but be servants to one another
in love. For the whole law can be summed up in a single
commandment: 'Love your neighbour as yourself.' But if you
go on fighting one another, tooth and nail, all you can expect is
mutual destruction" (Galatians 5:13–15 NEB). Mutual destruction is what we have seen in far too many male-female
relationships. And the reason for mutual destruction is the
failure to be servants to one another in love.

The Old Testament prophet Joel looked forward to a day
when the spirit of God would be poured out upon all flesh so
that men and women alike would prophesy (Joel 2:28–30). On
the day of Pentecost when the Holy Spirit came upon the
church, Peter stood up and announced that on that very day
Joel's prophecy had been fulfilled. Denying that the spirit-
filled Christians were drunk, Peter said: "No, this is what was

spoken by the prophet Joel: 'In the last days, God says, / I will pour out my Spirit on all people. / Your sons and daughters will prophesy, / your young men will see visions, / and your old men will dream dreams. / Even on my servants, both men and women, / I will pour out my Spirit in those days, / and they will prophesy" (Acts 2:16–18 NIV). In this passage, *to prophesy* does not carry the meaning of foretelling the future but rather of making public expositions of what the spirit of God teaches.[2] In other words, Peter is saying that both men and women have been empowered to *preach*.

The implications are enormous. Peter is announcing that the advent of the Holy Spirit has brought the end of patriarchal limitations upon the ministry of women. God does not discriminate on the basis of race, sex, or economic status in the distribution of spiritual gifts. The Christian community is compared to a human body in which "in each of us the Spirit is manifested in one particular way, for some useful purpose." One person "has the gift of wise speech, while another, by the power of the same Spirit, can put the deepest knowledge into words. Another, by the same Spirit, is granted faith; another, by the one Spirit, gifts of healing, and another miraculous powers. . . . But all these gifts are the work of one and the same Spirit, distributing them separately to each individual at will" (I Corinthians 12:7–11 NEB).

How can we tell which person should exercise which gift in the body or church of Christ? By paying attention to the talents which the Spirit has given to each person. Then how can we tell whether a woman should become an ordained preacher or teacher or priest? By consulting the gifts which each individual woman has been given, just as we would do with the male members of Christ's Body!

If a woman has been called and gifted by God to be a pastor or a priest, it is a fearful thing for the organized church to block her from that ministry. And if a Christian wife has been called and gifted for some career outside the home, and her husband blocks her by refusing to assist with the care of their mutual home and their mutual children, isn't he frustrating the work of the Holy Spirit? Dominance of the female in church and home places the male in a position of terrific spiritual danger.

Richard D. Kahoe, chairman of the Psychology Department at Georgetown College, has done a study of sexism and the human personality which has revealed that it is psychologically unhealthy for both women and men to favor female subordination. Conventionally submissive women tend to be self-protective, risk-avoiding, resistant to change, and maladjusted. "Men who oppose equality for women tend to be more authoritarian and non-conforming, higher in general neuroticism and need for power, and less reflective and self-reliant." In addition to his own findings with ninety-two college students, Dr. Kahoe cites three separate studies by Centers, Goldberg, and Worrell, each of which arrives at similar conclusions. Kahoe questions, "Since Egalitarianism is healthy, can a church be justified in denying equality to its women? Or . . . can a church be healthy that denies women [their human equality]?"[3] And, we might add, can a male-female relationship be healthy which proceeds on the patriarchal pattern of dominance and submission? As is so often the case, obedience to a biblical principle—in this case, the mutual submission and mutual service of male and female—is the best road to psychological health and positive human relationships.

For over ten years, people representing many different religious denominations have met together in an organization called the Evangelical Women's Caucus. Each year they have supported the following proposal: "We acknowledge that we have encouraged men to prideful domination and women to irresponsible passivity. So we call both men and women to mutual submission and active discipleship." Clearly that proposal is an expression of a new order, a new world, a New

Creation, a New Humanity. Ephesians 4:2–13 (NIV) describes the ideal for every one of us, male and female, in our individual lifestyle and in our relating to one another: "Be completely humble and gentle, be patient, bearing with one another in love. Make every effort to keep the unity of the Spirit through the bond of peace . . . so that the body of Christ may be built up until we all reach unity in the faith . . . and become mature, attaining the full measure of perfection found in Christ."

Here in the late twentieth century, we can find guidance in the timeless but frequently ignored principles of the Bible. As New Creatures in the Christ-nature we can resist the patriarchal principle of dominance and submission, with love serving one another. In this way we can embody Good News for a culture torn with the miserable results of human selfishness. Through mutual submission and mutual service we can begin to make the prayer of Jesus come true (John 17:21): "that all of them may be one."

Notes

1: The Christian Way of Relating

1. Leviticus 15:19–33; 12:1–5. For a brief but brilliant discussion of woman's status in Old Testament times which stresses more than I do the secondary and derivative female roles depicted there, see Rosemary Ruether, "Sexism and Liberation: The Historical Experience," in *From Machismo to Mutuality: Woman-Man Liberation*, by Eugene C. Bianchi and Rosemary Radford Ruether (Paramus, N.J.: Paulist Press, 1976).

2. The Talmud is a lengthy explanation and amplification of the Torah, the first five books of the Old Testament. The first part of the Talmud is a six-section code of law called the Mishnah, dating from about A.D. 200. The Mishnah includes all the legal developments in Judaism from the time of the Torah and is thus a good index to what society was like at the place and time of Jesus. For easily available further information concerning the rabbinical tradition and related topics, see Abraham Cohen, *Everyman's Talmud* (New York: Schocken Books, 1975); *The Essential Philo*, ed. Nahum N. Glatzer (New York: Schocken Books, 1971); David M. Feldman, *Marital Relations, Birth Control, and Abortion in Jewish Law* (New York: Schocken Books, 1974): and W. D. Davies, *Paul and Rabbinic Judaism* (New York: Harper & Brothers, 1948).

3. For a thorough study of the Bible on this topic, see Dwight Small, *The Right to Remarry* (Old Tappan, N. J.: Fleming H. Revell, 1975).

2: The Patriarchal Way of Relating

1. Vern L. Bullough (Urbana: University of Illinois Press, 1973); Elizabeth Gould Davis (New York: G. P. Putnam's Sons, 1971). Both books are now available in Penguin paperback.

2. *Protestant Biblical Interpretation* (Boston: W. A. Wilde Co., 1956), p. 17.

3. (New York: McGraw-Hill Book Co., 1976), pp. 245, 214.

4. *The Christian's Handbook of Psychiatry* (Old Tappan, N.J.: Fleming H. Revell, 1971), p. 162. Much of the material in the remainder of this chapter was first published in my article entitled "The Total Submission Woman," *Christian Herald*, 98 (November, 1975), 26–30.

5. *The Total Woman* (Old Tappan, N.J.: Fleming H. Revell, 1973), p. 80.

6. (St. Louis: Bethany Press, 1975), pp. 51, 151.

7. (Palo Alto, Calif.: Pacific Press, 1965). Now available in Bantam paperback.

8. (St. Louis: Bethany Press, 1970), p. 51.

9. Darien B. Cooper (Wheaton, Ill.: Victor Books, 1975); Jill Renich (Grand Rapids: Zondervan Publishing House, 1975); (Old Tappan, N.J.: Fleming H. Revell, 1972).

10. (Waco, Tex.: Word Books, 1975).

11. (Grand Rapids: Zondervan Publishing House, 1959), p. 100; (Grand Rapids: Zondervan Publishing House, 1972), p. 96.

12. (Chicago: Moody Press, 1975), pp. 33, 38.

13. *A Christian View of Men's and Women's Roles in a Changing World* (Family '76 Incorporated, 1975), p. 20.

14. *The Banner* (June 20, 1975), p. 11.

15. *McCalls*, 102 (June, 1975), 116.

16. Renich, *You Can Be the Wife of a Happy Husband*, p. 19.

17. *Total Woman*, p. 144; Wright, *Communication: The Key to Your Marriage* (Glendale, California: Regal, 1974), p. 90.

3: Is God Masculine?

1. Margaret Hannay, "C. S. Lewis: Mere Misogyny?" *Daughters of Sarah*, 1 (September, 1975), 1–4.

2. *That Hideous Strength* (New York: The Macmillan Co., 1965), p. 315.

3. Gershom Scholem, *On the Kabbalah and Its Symbolism* (New York: Schocken Books, 1965), pp. 159–65. See also Joseph B. Soloveitchik, *Tradition*, 7 (Summer, 1965), 5–6.

4. Letha Scanzoni and Nancy Hardesty, *All We're Meant to Be* (Waco, Tex.: Word Books, 1974), p. 56.

5. *The Torah: A Modern Commentary. Genesis*. Commentary by Gunther Plaut (New York: Union of Hebrew Congregations, 1974, p. 5.

6. J. Edgar Bruns, *God as Woman, Woman as God* (New York: Paulist Press, 1973), pp. 39–40.

7. For a fascinating but difficult Freudian discussion of biblical symbols surrounding the Godhead, see Ernest Jones, *Essays in Applied Psychoanalysis*, vol. II (New York: International Universities Press, 1964).

4: Freedom from Stereotypes

1. (New York: Walker and Company, 1969). *The Left Hand of Darkness* is now available in paperback from Ace Books.

2. See Phyllis Chesler, *Women and Madness* (Garden City, N.Y.: Doubleday & Co., 1972).

3. *The Brothers System for Liberated Love and Marriage* (New York: Peter H. Wyden, 1972), pp. 13–14. Some of the material in this chapter was first published in Virginia R. Mollenkott, "The Women's Movement Challenges the Church," *Journal of Psychology and Theology*, 2 (Fall, 1974), 298–310.

4. Letha and John Scanzoni, *Men, Women, and Change*, p. 15.

5. Roy G. D'Andrade, "Sex Differences and Cultural Institutions," in *The Development of Sex Differences* (Stanford: Stanford University Press, 1966), pp. 174–204.

6. I first ran across this information in a tabloid (*The National Tattler* [January 25, 1976], p. 3). I have since corroborated the information with Ms. Hidong K. Kwon, a Korean who holds a B.A. from Yonsei University (Seoul, Korea) and an M.L.S. from Colum-

bia University. Ms. Kwon comments: "Korea is a very traditional society. Therefore, Koreans do not want to admit in official sources that there is an island just off the tip of their country where everything is different." Lack of official information regarding sex roles in Cheju Island dramatizes one of the basic problems of women's studies: because women have been regarded as unimportant, their history has been largely unrecorded. Modern women, therefore, are finding it necessary to reconstruct their history inch by inch.

7. *Sex and Temperament* (New York: William Morrow & Co., 1935).

8. *Psychology Today* (September, 1975), p. 62.

9. *The Psychology of Consciousness* (New York: Viking Press, 1972), p. 225.

10. As quoted by Adrienne Rich in a review of *Women and Madness, New York Times Book Review* (December 21, 1972), p. 20.

11. "Theology and Womankind," *America*, 134 (January 17, 1976), 35.

5: Pauline Contradictions and Biblical Inspiration

1. See *Five Sermons and a Tract by Luther Lee*, ed. Donald W. Dayton (Chicago: Holrad House, 1975), which clarifies the role of the American Wesleyan Methodists in the Christian effort toward social justice.

2. "Woman," *Encyclopedia Judaica* (New York: The Macmillan Co., 1971).

3. Judith Hauptman, "Images of Women in the Talmud," *Religion and Sexism*, ed. Rosemary Ruether (New York: Simon & Schuster, 1974), p. 187.

4. The King James Version and *The Living Bible* read, "Nymphas, and to those who meet in *his* home." But the Revised Standard Version, The New English Bible, The New Testament in Modern English, The Jerusalem Bible, and other versions read, "Nympha and the church in *her* house."

5. Walter M. Abbott, *et al.*, *The Bible Reader: An Interfaith Interpretation* (New York: Bruce Books, 1969), p. 855.

6. The author is Dr. Paul Jewett, professor of systematic theology at Fuller Seminary. *Man as Male and Female* (Grand Rapids: Eerdmans Publishing Co., 1975).

7. *Reflections on the Psalms* (New York: Harcourt, Brace, and World, 1958).

8. *The Letters of Paul: Conversations in Context* (Atlanta: John Knox, 1975), p. 101.

6: Learning to Interpret Accurately

1. *Protestant Biblical Interpretation* (Boston: W. A. Wilde, 1956), pp. 102–3. For further help in accurate Bible study, see William Barclay, *Introducing the Bible* (Nashville: Abingdon Press, 1972); the chapter on "Revelation and the Bible" in John Lawson, *An Evangelical Faith for Today* (Nashville: Abingdon Press, 1972); and Peter Macky, *The Bible in Dialogue with Modern Man* (Waco, Tex.: Word Books, 1970).

7: Bible Doctrines and Human Equality

1. *Redbook,* 146 (February, 1976), 128.

2. See *Young's Analytical Concordance* (Grand Rapids: Associated Publishers and Authors, n.d.), p. 779.

3. "The Psychology and Theology of Sexism," *Journal of Psychology and Theology,* 2 (Fall, 1974), 284–90.

A Six-Session Study Guide
for Groups or Individuals

Session One:
Women, Men, and the Bible

HOW TO PREPARE FOR SESSION ONE

You will need the following for each person in your group: a Bible, a pencil or pen, and a note pad or paper with something to lean it on so that writing is comfortable.

Summary of Major Ideas in Session One (For use of group leaders only. Individuals should not read the summary until after doing all exercises.)

Much confusion exists concerning the role of women in the church and the home, and, of course, the role of male and female is interrelated. Because of the widespread confusion, it is important to study the Bible's message concerning male-female roles and relationships.

In order to begin with a clear profile of our own attitudes, a true-false quiz might be helpful. [**For quiz and post-quiz exercise, see special instructions below**].

The Bible is God's inspired word to our time and to every time.

[Read aloud Luke 13:10–21. See special instructions below.] The religious leader's attitude reflects the cheapness of human life, since animal needs but not human needs could transcend religious rulings.

Jesus violated many religious taboos in his treatment of the woman in Luke 13.

By defining the kingdom of God with one male and one female illustration, Jesus implied that bringing about God's will on earth is equally the task of male and female.

The low status of woman in the first century is reflected in Ecclesiasticus 25:24–26 (NEB): "Woman is the origin of sin, / and it is through her that we all die. / Do not leave a leaky cistern to drip / or allow a bad wife to say what she likes. / If she does not accept your control, divorce her and send her away."

In Matthew 19, Jesus rebuked the double standard of morality by contrasting the divorce law recorded in Deuteronomy 24:1–4 with God's original intention for male and female as recorded in Genesis 1 and 2.

And whereas Ecclesiasticus 25 called Eve the origin of sin, Genesis 3:20 called her the origin of life.

[Read aloud Luke 11:27–28. See special instructions below.]

Jesus blessed his mother not because of her anatomy but because of her spiritual attitudes and practices.

As Margaret Mead points out, contemporary turmoil is forcing people to learn to regard marriage and parenthood as special vocations rather than as the expected pattern for everyone.

Jesus traveled with women disciples (Luke 8:1–3), and, by his treatment of the hemorrhaging woman, he showed that the taboos against female bleeding (recorded in Leviticus 12 and 15) were no longer in operation.

Jesus also delivered to women some of his most important truths; see John 4:24 and John 20:17.

[**Read Mark 10:35–45. See special instructions below.**]

Jesus taught in Matthew 23:1–12 and in many other places that greatness is demonstrated by servanthood and that no Christian is ever intended to lord it over anyone else. [**Read Matthew 23:1–12. See special instructions below.**]

Although the New Testament teaches that Christians are intended to prefer and serve one another, society has taught us to expect women to serve and defer to men but not for men to serve and defer to women—at least, not in important matters like career relocation or the care of sick children in the middle of the night.

[**Read Ephesians 5:15–33. See special instructions below.**] Ephesians 5, which compares the role of the Christian husband to Jesus' self-giving, instructs husbands to lead the way in submission and loving concern, to which Christian wives respond with equally submissive and loving concern.

Ephesians 5:23 seems to use the word *head* in the sense of "source": the husband's loving self-giving is the source of the wife's, just as Christ's self-giving love is the source of the church's.

Special Instructions for Session One

FOR THE QUIZ. *GROUP:* If you are leading a group, see that everyone has writing equipment, then read the full instructions and quiz questions aloud slowly and clearly. People need not write down each question, but you should be sure that everyone in your group has numbered and answered each question before you move on to the next. *INDIVIDUAL:* Take the quiz on your own sheet of paper, being sure to read over the full instructions before answering.

THE QUIZ ITSELF: The group leader will read a series of statements; as they are read, mark down *True* or *False* according to your own beliefs. If you are not sure, take a guess because even a guess will give you some indication of your own assumptions. If you think the statement should usually be true, but perhaps not always true, mark it True anyway; if you think the statement should usually be false, although perhaps not always false, mark it False. Ready?

_____ 1. Most women are inferior to most men in intellectual and moral qualities.

_____ 2. The Bible teaches that most women are inferior to most men in intellectual and moral qualities.

_____ 3. Women should be silent in church services.

_____ 4. The Bible teaches that women should be silent in church services.

_____ 5. Women should not assume positions of authority over men.

_____ 6. The Bible teaches that women should not assume positions of authority over men.

_____ 7. Wives should obey their husbands.

_____ 8. The Bible teaches that wives should obey their husbands.

_____ 9. Husbands should obey their wives.

_____ 10. The Bible teaches that husbands should obey their wives.

_____ 11. Husbands and wives should be mutually submissive to each other, each one serving the other.

_____ 12. The Bible teaches that husbands and wives should be mutually submissive to each other, each one serving the other.

_____ 13. Married women should be full-time housekeepers and mothers.

_____ 14. The Bible teaches that married women should be full-time housekeepers and mothers.

_____ 15. God is masculine.

_____ 16. The Bible teaches that God is masculine.

_____ 17. I believe that the Bible is the inspired Word of God.

_____ 18. If I were shown that biblical teaching is the opposite of any of my opinions, I would change my opinions.

FOR POST-QUIZ EXERCISE. *GROUP:* The leader should read aloud the questions one by one, with their numbers, asking group members to share where they stand on each issue. It is important that there be no *arguing* about the issues but rather a clear *defining* of where each person stands. Also, group members should be asked to comment on their own consistency: if number 17 is marked True, 18 should also be marked True, and answers concerning one's own opinion and what the Bible teaches on the topic should all match each other. *INDIVIDUAL:* Think about your own answers to see if they are consistent with each other, following the instructions in the previous sentence. *BOTH INDIVIDUAL AND GROUP MEMBERS:* Save your answers, and after each session write down any evidence you find to *support* or *refute* the answers you have given.

FOR LUKE 13:10–21. *GROUP:* After reading the passage aloud, ask group members to define the attitude of the religious leaders as opposed to the attitude of Jesus. Also ask the group to discuss why Jesus used *two* illustrations, one male and one female, concerning the nature of God's realm. *INDIVIDUAL:* Think through the issues described in the previous sentences.

FOR LUKE 11:27–28. *GROUP:* After reading the passage aloud, ask group members to give their opinions about the implications of what Jesus says there. Specifically discuss whether Jesus would agree with Sigmund Freud that "anatomy is destiny." *INDIVIDUAL:* Think carefully through the issues mentioned above.

FOR MARK 10:35–45. *GROUP:* As the leader, do your best to get your group members imaginatively involved in their personal reactions to James and John's request in this passage.

If the group is uninhibited, let people play the roles of James, John, and Jesus while others pretend to overhear their request for special power in God's realm. Whether your group role-plays or simply reads the passage aloud, afterward, try to get each group member to describe his or her feelings upon hearing other people ask to outrank them in the realm they are all working together to establish. Finally, try to get each member to describe his or her honest reactions to Jesus' reply. What principle is Jesus teaching? Does each person believe it? Practice it? Would each of you have actually heard the principle, or would you have been too busy watching James and John get put in their place? *INDIVIDUAL:* Try to imagine each aspect of the group exercise, and study your own reactions.

FOR MATTHEW 23:1–12. *GROUP:* After having members of the group read the passage aloud, ask them to make two parallel columns on a sheet of paper, one describing the religious leaders' way of relating, the other describing Jesus' concept of relating, as this passage pictures each of them. Then lead the group in a sharing of their lists and an honest assessment of the human relationships in their own home, church, and place of business. Which column do those relationships more closely resemble? *INDIVIDUAL:* Follow the instructions for the group, except that you will have to do your own private job of assessing whether relationships in your home, church, and place of business are more like those of the religious leaders or more like the ones Jesus approves.

FOR EPHESIANS 5:15–33. *GROUP:* After the reading, get your group members to tell why they think Paul leans on the verb in verse 21 ("submit yourselves") when he writes verse 22. In other words, why didn't Paul repeat the verb *to submit?* Why did he make the verb for wifely submission depend on the verb for universal Christian submission? What does this imply about human relating within marriage? Also ask the group members to describe what *aspect* of Christ's experience the husband's role is related to. *INDIVIDUAL:* Think through all aspects of the group exercise.

Between Now and the Second Session

Try to get in touch with your real *feelings* about male-female equality in the New Humanity. Read carefully Philippians 2:5–8, preferably in several different translations. If you are male, ask yourself whether, in the light of this passage, serving and deferring to women should make you feel degraded. If you are female, ask yourself whether, in the light of Philippians 2, it is right for married women to make all the emotional adjustments and do all the giving in. Might this not amount to depriving men of the opportunity to become Christlike? Whether you are male or female, what sort of *balance* do you think would be wise to achieve in your own relationships with the other sex?

Session Two:
Patriarchal Versus Christian Ways of Relating

HOW TO PREPARE FOR SESSION TWO

For this session each member of your group will need only a Bible. Do not worry whether the translations are different; it is valuable to compare various translations with one another.

Summary of Major Ideas in Session Two (For use of group

leaders only. Individuals should not read the summary until after doing the exercises.)

All of the New Testament passages concerning wifely submission are set in a context of universal Christian submission and compassionate concern: for instance, I Peter 2:9–3:8. [Read I Peter 2:9–3:8 aloud. See special instructions below.]

Some people claim that slavery was a first-century practice that cannot be countenanced in the twentieth-century; yet they argue that the subordination of wife to husband is *not* just a cultural practice but is intended as a rule for all places and all times. But the passage in I Peter makes that distinction impossible. First-century slaves were told to obey their masters because of Christ's example, while first-century wives were told to accept the authority of their husbands *"in the same way."* The reason for such submission was the same in each case: so that unbelievers would be won over to Christianity.

Both Peter and Paul used language of submission concerning wives and language of love concerning husbands because of the cultural conditions of their times, in which husbands had absolute power and control over their wives. Their first concern was to win people to Christ.

Yet Peter and Paul always spoke of the slave's and the Christian wife's submission in the context of universal Christian submission. Therefore, had Christian principles actually been *obeyed,* the institution of slavery and the male domination of women would have ended within one generation. [Reread I Peter 3:7. See special instructions below.]

Only when we put ourselves into the skin of a first-century husband newly converted to Christianity can we begin to understand how revolutionary the words of Peter and Paul must have sounded. Because the wives were the weaker, more vulnerable partners in first-century marriages, Peter orders that they should be *honored.* And Peter wipes out traditional assumptions about female intellectual and moral inferiority by speaking of women as the spiritual equals of their husbands.

In strong contrast stands the advice being given to Christian men and women in many recent books which claim to be biblical. [**See special instructions concerning the quotation from Larry Christenson.**]

Although Christenson counsels reverence and obedience toward abusive husbands, the apostle Paul in I Corinthians 7:10–11 allows for the possibility that an abused Christian wife may separate from her husband. And while Christenson will allow husbands to correct their wives while wives must suffer in silence, both Peter and Paul counsel *oneness* and *mutual* submission and concern for those Christians who happen to be married to each other.

Marabel Morgan's *The Total Woman* (Old Tappan, N. J.: Fleming H. Revell, 1973) and many other books in the same vein counsel Christian wives to be totally and unconditionally submissive to their husbands. [**See special instructions concerning the quotation from Judith M. Miles.**]

Mrs. Miles, like Mrs. Darien B. Cooper in *You Can Be the Wife of a Happy Husband* (Wheaton, Ill.: Victor Books, 1974, p. 91), argues that even should the Christian husband commit adultery, the Christian wife should not swerve in her submission and absolute trust.

These total-submission books imply that obedience to the husband supplies a moral shield for the wife; but Acts 5:1–11 refutes any such notion, since Sapphira received the same punishment as her husband for lying to the Lord.

We are dealing with the marriage relationship, not because every Christian person ought to be married but because marriage undergirds male-female relationships elsewhere in society. Unmarried persons may easily apply similar principles to their own relationships.

Book after book assumes that the husband's needs are primary, the wife's secondary—for instance, Jill Renich's *To Have and To Hold* (Grand Rapids: Zondervan, 1972) even argues that Christian wives must submit to marital relations when they are not interested (p. 59). But Paul sees things differently. [**Read aloud I Corinthians 7:3–5. See special instructions below.**]

[**See special instructions concerning the second Judith M. Miles quotation and the reading of Genesis 1:26–28 and Galatians 3:28.**] In the original creation, male and female were given equal dominion over the rest of creation (Genesis 1:26–28); and in the New Creation, all sexual prejudice is to be broken down in the unity of Christ's one Body (Galatians 3:28).

Not surprisingly, what the Bible teaches is also the *healthiest* form of male-female relating. Domination of one person by another leads to loss of energy in them both; mutual concern with honest communication leads to new energy in both partners.

Although the world teaches that one must lose so that another can win, Jesus teaches relationships in which both people win.

Special Instructions for Session Two

FOR I PETER 2:9–3:8. *GROUP:* As the passage is read aloud, ask your group to pay special attention to the way the thought flows from one segment of society to another. Then try to get people to commit themselves concerning how much I Peter 3:8 is intended to govern the rest of the instructions. In other words, if *all* Christians are supposed to be "kindly and humble-minded," are wives supposed to be *more so* than their husbands? If not, why do both Peter and Paul use language of *submission* concerning wives but speak of love rather than submission on the part of husbands? This would be a good time to review the group's recollection of first-century cultural conditions to see whether those conditions account for the difference in Peter and Paul's language concerning husbands and wives. *INDIVIDUAL:* Carefully think through all the issues raised in the group instructions.

FOR THE RE-READING OF I PETER 3:7. *GROUP:* Ask each person in your group to close his or her eyes and imagine that he or she is a first-century *male* who has just been converted to Christianity—has been married for years before conversion, but is now hearing for the first time how Christians are supposed to treat their wives. After everyone has had a few seconds to get into that imaginative frame of mind, read I Peter 3:7 slowly and with great emphasis. Then let each group member tell what feelings he or she has, listening to that verse *through the ears of a first-century married man.* *INDIVIDUAL:* Let your imagination place you back in the first century in a male body as you read and react to I Peter 3:7.

READ THE QUOTATION FROM LARRY CHRISTENSON.

In the case of a Christian wife with a tyrannical husband, the position of the wife, according to God's ordinance, is not in the least altered. . . . Her duty toward her husband remains exactly the same; she is none the less bound to pay him reverence than if his character had been the gentlest and the most enlightened. . . . As certain as the marriage bond is indissoluble, so certainly the command of obedience in marriage stands irrevocably firm. . . . She *must* see Christ in her husband.
—Christenson, *The Christian Family* (Minneapolis: Bethany Fellowship, 1970), p. 52.

GROUP: Try to get every member in your group, male and female, to put himself or herself into the shoes of the woman and to imagine and describe his or her reactions to receiving the above advice from Pastor Christenson. *INDIVIDUAL:* Let your imagination place you in the body of the woman described by Christenson; *feel* the abuse heaped upon you by your tyrannical husband, and then listen to and react to Pastor Christenson's advice.

READ THE QUOTATION FROM JUDITH M. MILES:

> Just as I can trust God completely because of His nature, I can trust my husband unreservedly. Whether or not he is worthy of trust is between him and God; it is not my concern or responsibility. . . . If a wholly trusted husband were to sin in adultery, I am sure the Christian wife would be deeply grieved. . . . But I am sure that God would supply the grace of forgiveness, and the husband might be wholly trusted still.
>
> —Miles, *The Feminine Principle* (Minneapolis: Bethany Fellowship, 1975), p. 85

GROUP: Ask your group members to split into *pairs* and to tell each other their honest answers to the following questions: (1) Do I *want* to be trusted as if I were God? Why or why not? (2) Do I want my most intimate friend (if I am married, my mate) to say that my moral condition is not his or her concern? Why or why not? *INDIVIDUAL:* Look directly into your own eyes in a mirror and answer the above questions as completely as possible.

FOR I CORINTHIANS 7:3–5. *GROUP:* After the reading, define exactly which partner Paul identifies as the boss in physical matters. *Prove* what your group decides by referring to the details of the text. *INDIVIDUAL:* List for yourself the exact details that lead you to whatever conclusion you reach concerning Paul's attitude toward marital leadership in physical relating.

READ THE SECOND QUOTATION FROM JUDITH M. MILES AND GENESIS 1:26–28 AND GALATIANS 3:28.

As the wife decreases, the husband increases. Conversely, if

the wife does not decrease, or if she increases herself, the husband is thwarted or diminished. In effect I am postulating a closed system composed of a man and a woman with a finite amount of energy. If the family energy is concentrated in a man's career, the family unit will rise and accelerate along whatever course it is taking. Inertia and drag are eliminated through the persistent helping of the unselfish wife.
—Miles, *The Feminine Principle,* p. 99

GROUP: After rereading the Miles quotation and having someone read aloud from Genesis and Galatians, compare what Mrs. Miles says with what the Bible says about the relative importance and authority of male and female. Try to get *everyone* talking. *INDIVIDUAL:* Compare Mrs. Miles' assumptions with those of the authors of Genesis and Galatians.

Between Now and the Third Session

Please read chapters 1 and 2 of *Women, Men, and the Bible.* Try to make your learning practical by developing a personal approach to others on a both-win or both-lose basis. When you become involved in differences of opinion, try exchanging points of view; attempt to state the other person's position until he or she is satisfied, while the other person attempts to state your position and is corrected in it until you feel the statement is accurate. If you keep at this until each of you feels satisfied and then try to reach a compromise solution in which *both* of you feel you've been heard and understood and considered, you will notice a flow of new energy. Once you have felt this energy, you will never want to go back to the patriarchal "dominance and submission" way of relating.

Session Three:
Is God Masculine?

HOW TO PREPARE FOR SESSION THREE

You will need a chalkboard and chalk, and for each person in your group there should be a Bible, a pencil or pen, and a note pad or paper with something to lean it on so that writing is comfortable. At least one Bible should contain a *concordance*.

Summary of Major Ideas in Session Three (For use of group leaders only. Individuals should not read the summary until after doing all exercises.)

No matter how intelligent they may be, most people don't question their assumption that God is masculine. Many factors in society and in the Bible cause us to think of God in masculine terms.

[See special instructions for the exercise concerning God and masculinity.] We think of God as masculine because: (1) all the biblical pronouns concerning God are masculine; (2) Jesus told us that we should pray "Our *Father*"; (3) Jesus was the "express image of God's person," according to Hebrews 1:3, and Jesus was male; (4) in most of Jesus' parables, the figure of God is masculine; (5) in the Old Testament, God is referred to as both a father and a husband to his people Israel; (6) we associate God with kingship and authority and control, and in our society such power is associated with men rather than with women; (7) almost all preachers and church dignitaries and famous spiritual leaders are male.

[See special instructions for the exercise concerning feminine images for the First Person of the Trinity.] The Bible frequently speaks of God the "Father" in terms of female roles and personhood; for instance, see Genesis 3:21; Nehemiah 9:21; Numbers 11:12; Hosea 11; Psalm 22:9; Psalm 71:6; Job 3:2; Isaiah 46:3–4; Isaiah 66:9; Isaiah 42:14; Isaiah 49:15; Isaiah 66:3; Psalm 131:1–2; Luke 15:8–10. This discovery better enables us to understand Genesis 1:26–28, which says that the female as well as the male was made in the image of God.

Of course, when the Second Person was incarnated as a human being, it was as a male; but the first-century culture made that a historical necessity. What does matter a great deal is that New Testament authors referred to Jesus not with the Greek word *aner*, "male," but rather with the Greek word *anthropos*, "human being." And John 1 tells us that the Word was made *flesh*. Jesus also spoke of himself as a mother hen (Matthew 23:37 and Luke 13:34–35). He manifested traits that Jewish society labeled "feminine" as well as those it labeled "masculine." And he was closely associated with the masculine Greek concept of *Logos* (John 1) which in turn is closely associated with the feminine Hebrew concept of *Wisdom* (Proverbs 8, etc.). Thus Jesus embodied the perfection of both male and female humanity in order to provide salvation for both male and female humanity.

[**See special instructions concerning the quotation from the Wisdom of Solomon.**] The passage from Wisdom of Solomon pictures the feminine personification of wisdom in images that clearly apply also to the Sovereign Jesus Christ as portrayed in the New Testament. Among the points of clear contact are the following: (1) Wisdom is equated with the Word of God; Jesus is equated both to the wisdom of God, I Corinthians 1:24, and to the Word of God, John 1:1. (2) Wisdom moves through all things; in the Christ all of us have our being (Acts 17:28). (3) Wisdom is the image of God; the Christ is "the express image of God's person" (Hebrews 1:3 and John 12:44). (4) Wisdom is unchanging; Jesus Christ is the same yesterday, today, and forever (Hebrews 13:8). (5) Wisdom makes all things new; the Christ makes all things new (Revelation 21:5). (6) Wisdom orders all things benignly; all things consist in and will be reconciled to the Christ (Colossians 1:16 and 20). (7) Wisdom is the active cause of all things; the Christ is the maker of all things (John 1:3 and Colossians 1:16). (8) Wisdom sits beside God's throne; the Christ sits at the right hand of God (Hebrews 1:3, etc.). (9) Wisdom was present with God at the making of the world; the Christ was "in the beginning with God" (John 1:2). (10) Wisdom is sent forth from the holy heavens to come down to earth; the Christ was made flesh to dwell among us (John 1:14). (11) Wisdom is the only way to know God's will, the only way to become acceptable to God; the Christ reveals God's will to us (John 12:49), and being in the Christ-nature is the only way for human beings to become acceptable to God (John 14:6). (12) Wisdom is everlasting light; the Christ is the light of the world (John 1:4; John 12:46; etc.). (13) Wisdom sets humanity on the right path; Jesus identified himself as "*the way*, the truth, and the life" (John 14:6).

It is clear from all the feminine imagery surrounding Jesus that Jesus is intended to be thought of as *fully human* rather than as exclusively masculine.

[See special instructions for the exercise concerning the feminine images for the Third Person of the Trinity.] In John 3, Jesus spoke of the Holy Spirit as the mother of all who have been born again; in John 7:37–39 he identifies the Spirit with the feminine image of "streams of living water"; and in John 14 Jesus pictures the Spirit as the comforter, the one "called alongside to help," a distinctly feminine role in Hebrew culture (remember that Eve was Adam's help sent from God).

Since Jesus spoke of all three persons of the Trinity in feminine as well as masculine terms, we must recognize that God transcends all human limitations and remains beyond our comprehension. John 4:24 tells us that God is spirit; so it is tragic that women have been relegated to second-class citizenship in the family of God because of the notion that God is masculine.

Through the centuries the Christian churches have failed to teach that biblical metaphors of God as Father are indeed metaphors, figures of speech, not to be taken literally. Our liturgies, hymns, prayers, and theological language have done very little to remind us of that truth.

[See special instructions for the exercise concerning the Christmas carol.] Excluding feminine images from the language of Christian theology has for centuries made girls and women feel left out, forgotten, invisible.

In I Corinthians 9:22–23, the apostle Paul says he would be willing to become all things to all persons in order to win them to Christ. If our exclusion of the feminine in our God-language is keeping feminists away from the Christ, shouldn't we be willing to enter into the apostolic spirit enough to make our language more *inclusive?*

[See special instructions for the exercises concerning God-language.] A complete changeover to feminine images and forms of address to God is hardly necessary, but we should follow the biblical precedent of referring to God in feminine terms as well as masculine ones. We should also adapt the words of our hymns, liturgies, and prayers to make them more inclusive and therefore more loving. And of course we must also move beyond mere changes of language to practical changes in the power structure of our churches, homes, and places of business. As people of faith, we must try to bring about the will of God on earth as it is in heaven—and that would mean wiping out every vestige of racism, economic elitism, sexism, heterosexism, and other forms of prejudice.

Special Instructions for Session Three

FOR THE EXERCISE CONCERNING GOD AND MASCULINITY. *GROUP:* As leader, post yourself (or some member of the group) at the chalkboard. Then ask group members to suggest any factor they can think of that causes most people to think of God as masculine, including Bible stories, prayers, liturgies, or social patterns. Each factor should be written on the chalkboard as it is suggested. See the synopsis above for seven basic factors that you can suggest if the group gets bogged down. INDIVIDUAL: Make your own list on chalkboard or note pad.

FOR THE EXERCISE CONCERNING FEMININE IMAGES FOR THE FIRST PERSON OF THE TRINITY. GROUP: Again, with one person posted at the board to write down the results, ask each person to look through the Bible in search of passages that speak of God in ways that suggest maternity or femaleness rather than maleness. Someone should look in the concordance under woman, mother, and related topics to see whether any of the passages sound as if they might be referring to the First Person of the Trinity. Remind the group that delivering and caring for babies and feeding and clothing people were considered strictly "woman's work" in Hebrew society; so any pictures of God's fulfilling those roles would be maternal word-pictures. If the group bogs down, assign individuals to look up and read aloud the various references recorded in the summary above in connection with this topic. INDIVIDUAL: Follow the group instructions except, of course, that you will have to write down your own list.

FOR AN EXERCISE CONCERNING A QUOTATION FROM WISDOM OF SOLOMON. GROUP: Each group member should write down, as the passage is read, any detail he or she notices that sounds like the way Jesus is described in the New Testament. After hearing the passage several times in order to pick out the details that sound like Jesus, everyone should look in the New Testament, trying to pin down the specific passages that describe Jesus in terms that sound like Old Testament Wisdom. After everyone has shared these results in general discussion, try to get each person to tell how he or she *feels* about applying feminine pronouns (in the description of Wisdom) to the person of Jesus Christ. If your group bogs down, refer to the summary of this topic for suggestions you can make. *INDIVIDUAL:* Follow the group instructions as much as possible. Here is the passage, from Wisdom of Solomon 7:24–9:18 (NEB):

Wisdom moves more easily than motion itself, she pervades and permeates all things because she is so pure. . . . She is the brightness that streams from everlasting light, the flawless mirror of the active power of God and the image of [God's] goodness. She is but one, yet can do everything; herself unchanging, she makes all things new; age after age she enters into holy souls, and makes them God's friends and prophets, for nothing is acceptable to God but the [one] who makes [a] home with wisdom. . . . She spans the world in power from end to end, and orders all things benignly. . . . It is given to her to live with God. . . . What is richer than wisdom, the active cause of all things? . . . Who more than wisdom is the artificer of all that is? . . . God of our [ancestors], merciful Lord, who has made all things by thy word, and in thy wisdom hast fashioned [people], . . . give me wisdom, who sits beside thy throne, . . . wisdom, who is familiar with thy works and was present at the making of the world by thee, who knows what is acceptable to thee and in line with thy commandments. Send her forth from the holy heavens, and from thy glorious throne bid her come down. . . . Who ever learnt to know thy purposes, unless thou hadst given [that person] wisdom . . . ? Thus it was that those on earth were set upon the right path.

FOR AN EXERCISE CONCERNING FEMININE IMAGES FOR THE THIRD PERSON OF THE TRINITY. *GROUP:* Ask each member of the group to leaf through the Gospel of John, looking for places where Jesus refers to the

Spirit in terms that suggest femaleness: birth imagery, water imagery, imagery of giving comfort, and the like. Share by writing each discovery on the chalkboard. If the group bogs down, refer to the summary under this topic for some suggestions. *INDIVIDUAL:* Follow the group instructions.

FOR AN EXERCISE CONCERNING A CHRISTMAS CAROL. *GROUP:* As the carol is read, have group members count on their fingers the masculine and feminine references in the stanza; then have all contribute what they have noticed by tallying on the chalkboard all masculine references and feminine references. *INDIVIDUAL:* Make your own tally of masculine and feminine references and think about the implications.

> Hail the heaven-born Prince of Peace! Hail the Sun of Righteousness!
> Light and life to all he brings, Risen with healing in his wings.
> Mild he lays his glory by, Born that man no more may die,
> Born to raise the sons of earth, Born to give them second birth.
> Hark! the herald angels sing, "Glory to the new-born King!"

FOR THE EXERCISE CONCERNING GOD-LANGUAGE. *GROUP:* While someone summarizes each suggestion on the chalkboard, have group members make suggestions about practical ways women and girls can be made to feel more included in the family of God by making theological language more inclusive. You might take a specific hymn from your own church's hymnal and work as a group to eliminate the sexism; or you might work together on revising some section of a liturgy. Or you may prefer to keep the suggestions more general. You should also see to it that some of the suggestions move beyond language changes into concrete suggestions concerning changes in social patterns within the Christian community which would help to reflect the unity of male and female in the New Creation. Should more women be elected to important posts, etc.? *INDIVIDUAL:* Think through the above issues.

Between Now and Session Four

Please read chapter 3 of *Women, Men, and the Bible;* do all you can to make your own prayers and conversations inclusively human rather than unconsciously sexist. Try very deliberately to share your insights and action plans with members of your church or social group.

Session Four: Freedom from Stereotypes

HOW TO PREPARE FOR SESSION FOUR

You will need the following equipment for each person in your group: a Bible, a pencil or pen, and a note pad or paper with something to lean it on so that writing is comfortable.

Summary of Major Ideas in Session Four (For use of group leaders only. Individuals should not read the summary until after doing all exercises.)

Although many people assume that certain traits are forever masculine and others forever feminine, it is important to understand how such traits are acquired and what the Bible says about them.

In order to be clear about our own attitudes, a self-quiz is in order. [See special instructions for the self-quiz.]

Typically, the following traits are considered to be feminine: joyfulness, tendency to be loving and compassionate, passivity, willingness to be a follower, dependence, peacefulness, patience, gentleness, goodness (a kind, forgiving, and grateful nature), fidelity or faithfulness, temperance, and meekness or humility. And the following traits are typically more fully associated with the masculine: creativeness, tendency toward strong initiative, originality, independence, aggressiveness, egocentricity, selfishness, leadership, clear and logical thinking, assertiveness (self-assurance), emotional control, and strong powers of concentration.

Although some individuals may differ slightly from the above associations because of individual experiences, scrutiny of literature through the centuries and of popular attitudes today will bear out the masculine and feminine associations of each trait. For instance, in *The Bible's Legacy for Womanhood* (Garden City, N.Y.: Doubleday & Co. 1970; reprint ed., New York: Pillar Books, 1976), Edith Deen supports sex-role stereotypes by praising William Booth for his "masculine energy and foresight" and Catherine Booth for her "feminine tenderness and spiritual sensitivity."

[See special instructions concerning the exercise on individual traits.] Most people discover that their personalities do not completely conform to stereotypical thinking about what their sex is supposed to be like.

[See special instructions for sharing results concerning individual traits.] The technical name for possessing a mixture of psychological traits commonly associated with masculinity and femininity is *psychological androgyny.* If society could break free from its sexual stereotypes, of course, we would eventually be able to drop terms like *androgyny* and speak simply of *human* traits and full *personhood.* [See special instructions for the exercise concerning Galatians 5:22–23.] All the fruits of the Spirit listed in Galatians 5:22–23 are stereotypically associated with the feminine; yet Paul urged male as well as female Christians to develop those traits. If it were important for men and women to differ from each other in their psychological as well as their physical makeup, we can be sure the Bible would have urged certain traits upon women and certain other traits upon men.

Instead of following the New Testament, which teaches both males and females to become Christlike, Christians have followed the standards of secular society, encouraging men (the powerful class) to develop the traits of leaders and rulers and women (the dependent class) to develop the traits of those who follow and are ruled. The Christian virtues have been assigned to women so that men can feel free to compete in the arenas of fiscal and political power.

We learn sex roles by the process of socialization. From earliest childhood we receive hints about what our behavior patterns should be. These hints are reinforced at school, where textbooks picture boys in active, aggressive roles and girls in passive, secondary roles. And, in society itself, males continue to dominate every major institution: the church, the military, the national government, big business, science, law, and so forth. No wonder American women tend to see themselves as secondary to men!

[See special instructions for the exercise concerning personal socialization.] Genesis stories of creation make no differentiation of males as active and females as passive. According to Genesis 1:26–28, responsible rulership is a feminine role just as much as it is a masculine one. Only the androcentrism of our society has read *into* the Genesis text any suggestion of dominance and submission before the fall. Genesis Rabbah 18:2, a commentary included in the Talmud, makes clear that tradition interpreted the creation stories as teaching female subordination and inferiority. Thus the Genesis Rabbah helps us to understand how ideas of subordination came to surround and encrust a text that actually teaches no such thing.

[See special instructions for the exercise concerning I Corinthians 12:1–13 and 27–31.] According to this passage, all the gifts in the Christian community come from the Holy Spirit and are assigned to individuals without reference to race, sex, or economic status. This indicates clearly that in the Christian church, home, and business, the best way to determine God's will for each individual is to take notice of what gifts the Spirit has given to that individual. For instance, if a woman wants to be a priest and has the gifts needed for the priesthood, is it not God's will for her to be a priest?

Special Instructions for Session Four

FOR THE SELF-QUIZ. *GROUP:* Have everyone number a paper from 1 to 24, then write down the specific trait beside the appropriate number as it is dictated.

1. joyfulness
2. creativeness
3. tendency to be loving and compassionate
4. tendency toward strong initiative
5. passivity
6. willingness to be a follower
7. originality
8. independence
9. dependence
10. peacefulness
11. aggressiveness
12. egocentricity
13. patience
14. gentleness
15. goodness (a kind, forgiving, and grateful nature)
16. selfishness
17. leadership
18. fidelity (faith, or faithfulness)
19. temperance
20. meekness (humility)
21. clear, logical thinking
22. assertiveness (self-assurance)
23. emotional control
24. strong powers of concentration

When everyone has copied the above list, have people write down an *M* next to the trait if they associate that trait with males or an *F* if they associate the trait with females. If anybody associates the trait equally with males and females, he or she should answer in terms of what is probably the *typical* association most of his or her acquaintances would make. When everyone has marked every trait either *M* or *F*, spend a few minutes sharing results and trying to identify why the associations are as they are. *INDIVIDUAL:* Follow the group instructions, thinking through the reasons for the associations you make with each trait. [**Both group members and individuals working alone should save their lists for further use in this session.**]

FOR THE EXERCISE ON INDIVIDUAL TRAITS. *GROUP:* Ask each group member to make a star next to every trait that he or she recognizes as one of his or her personal traits most of the time. Pay no attention to the *M* or *F* designations for the time being; just concentrate on which traits describe your own behavior the majority of the time. *INDIVIDUAL:* Follow the group instructions.

FOR SHARING RESULTS CONCERNING INDIVIDUAL TRAITS: *GROUP:* Ask each group member to make a private tally of how many of his or her personal traits are stereotypically masculine and how many stereotypically feminine. The interesting thing here will be to find out how many "masculine" traits the women in your group feel they possess and vice versa. See if you can get group members to share their findings with one another and especially to describe their feelings about having traits that are stereotypically associated with the other sex. *INDIVIDUAL:* Follow the group instructions, trying to define your feelings about any characteristics you possess that are usually associated with the other sex.

FOR THE EXERCISE CONCERNING GALATIANS 5:22–23. *GROUP:* After reading aloud Galatians 5:22–23, ask each group member to underline each of the fruits of the Spirit on his or her list of traits. Then, as a group, count how many of the fruits of the Spirit are associated in modern society with masculinity, how many with femininity. As group leader, refer to the synopsis under this point for some suggestions about the implications of this exercise, and introduce those ideas if discussion should bog down. *INDIVIDUAL:* Follow group instructions, being sure to try to figure things out on your own before referring to the synopsis.

FOR THE EXERCISE ON PERSONAL SOCIALIZATION. *GROUP:* Give group members a chance to go over their list of traits to decide which traits they do *not* manifest most of the time but would *like* to manifest. If any of these traits are usually associated with the other sex, ask group members to talk about whether it is possible that fear of societal disapproval might have caused them to shy away from the trait. On the other hand, someone may be especially pleased about some trait which is his or her own, although it is usually associated with the other sex, and may be able to remember that some person influenced him or her to develop that trait, making it seem (by word or example) that such a trait was quite all right for him or her to develop. Try to get every person in the group to share at least one comment concerning one trait he or she would like to develop or is glad to have developed even though that trait is stereotypically associated with the other sex. The point of the exercise is to bring about the realization that desirable traits are *humanly* desirable and should not be limited to one sex only. *INDIVIDUAL:* Think about how you developed the traits you already manifest and which traits you would like to develop in the future. Try to picture yourself as a complete and perfect human being and then think about practical methods of moving toward that ideal.

FOR THE EXERCISE CONCERNING I CORINTHIANS 12:1–13 AND 27–31. *GROUP:* After the passage has been read aloud, discuss the implications for male-female relationships in church and home. How can you tell, according to this passage, whether certain roles should be reserved exclusively for one sex? According to this passage, who ought to decide who may perform specific functions in the church and in the home? As group leader, feel free to refer to the synopsis for suggestions to aid the discussion. Be sure to ask each person who contributes to the discussion to point out in the biblical text exactly what detail causes him or her to draw the conclusion that he or she is presenting. *INDIVIDUAL:* Think through the issues presented above, referring to the summary on this topic only after reaching your own conclusions.

Between Now and Session Five

Please read chapter 4 of *Women, Men, and the Bible*. Think deeply about your own gifts. Begin working actively on the development of one trait that you would like to manifest. Try this week to do at least one thing to encourage someone in your local church or social group to develop and use the gifts he or she possesses. Perhaps a word of appreciation will be just the right thing.

Session Five:
Interpreting the Bible

HOW TO PREPARE FOR THIS SESSION

It would be helpful for the group leader to bring to this session as many of the following scholarly tools as he or she can assemble: a good Bible dictionary, an analytical concordance, an interlinear translation, and a Bible verse-by-verse commentary. At the end of the session, group members should be encouraged to examine these tools. But the only equipment that is absolutely necessary is a Bible for each member of the group and a pen or pencil with a note pad or paper with something to lean it on so that writing is comfortable.

Summary of Major Ideas in Session Five (For use of group leaders only. Individuals should not read the summary until after doing all exercises.)

Concerning the interpretation of the Bible, church traditions tend toward either of two extremes: one which assumes that the Bible is so *simple* that it can be understood without the help of any scholarly tools; the other which assumes that the Bible is so *difficult* that only specialist scholars can interpret it.

In each of these traditions, what the particular church thinks that the Bible must mean is interposed between the individual reader and the biblical text.

In fact, the central message of the Bible, the message of God's love and human redemption, is simple, clear, and unbreakable. But the Bible is also a huge and complex book, and a full understanding of it requires a great deal of help from scholarly tools.

Since not all of us have time to go to seminary, yet all of us need to find daily guidance from the Bible, we might be helped by thinking about some principles of interpreting the Bible. [See special instructions for the exercise concerning principles of interpretation.]

The most practical way to check out the validity of the principles of interpretation is to apply them to a specific passage. [See special instructions for exercise concerning I Timothy 2:11–15.]

In many of the youth cults in contemporary America, the most extreme female subordination is practiced *in the name of the Bible;* so it is important for us to understand how to interpret properly the biblical text. Human happiness and health is involved.

Just as cultists have imagined a master-slave relationship between husband and wife on the basis of Ephesians 5 (which actually teaches *mutual* submission), they have forced women into submission on the basis of I Timothy 2:11–15. So it is a good passage for applying our principles of interpretation in order to check their validity. At the same time we can increase our own understanding of one of the most difficult passages in Scripture.

Principle 1 is valid. But those of us who do not know Hebrew, Greek, and Aramaic can find help in Bible commentaries, interlinear translations, and analytical concordances. [See special instructions for exercise concerning the situation at Ephesus.]

Principle 2 is valid. Apparently, at Ephesus, certain women were acting rude in local church meetings, interrupting the services, teaching confused doctrines, and publicly humiliating their husbands by lording it over them. Titus 1:10–11 tells us that a similar situation occurred among certain men on the island of Crete; but we do not use that passage to silence all men in all churches everywhere. [See special instructions concerning Galatians 3:28.] Because Galatians 3:28 is set in a *doctrinal* context, its sweeping aside of sexual barriers should take precedence over other passages on women in the church, which are set in the context of dealing with specific local problems.

Principle 3 is valid. Accordingly, the verb *authentein* should have been translated not "to have authority over men" but rather "to domineer over men," in accordance with contemporary Greek usage.

Principle 4 is valid. It is best to admit we do not know the meaning of the obscure phrase concerning salvation by childbearing in I Timothy 2:15.

Principle 5 is valid. Since the literal meaning of I Timothy 2:15 is obscure, it is dangerous to make the various applications of it which have sometimes been made.

Principle 6 is valid. [See special instructions for the exercise concerning authentein.]

The concepts of suicide, murdering one's family, and lordship or autocracy all have in common the idea of self-will and aggressive dominance. So I Timothy is not concerned with women with *earned* authority but rather with women who have *usurped* authority by acts of arbitrary self-will. Such unearned authority is wrong for any Christian, male or female.

Principle 7 is valid. The extremely repressive use of I Timothy 2:11–15 would have been curbed by faithfully interpreting it in the light of such broad doctrinal themes as the priesthood of all believers and the principle of New Creaturehood in the Christ.

Principle 8 is valid. But it is difficult to put aside the assumptions we have formed because of the socialization process to which we have been subjected. To free ourselves of our personal prejudices, biases, and traditions requires a constant alertness.

Principle 9 is valid. But for I Timothy 2:14 in English translations, no fully rational interpretation can be found.

Principle 10 is valid. Since hundreds of passages indicate that males as well as females are sinners, we cannot use I Timothy 2:14 to prove that only woman is a sinner; and since many passages make clear that salvation is through faith in Christ, we cannot deduce from I Timothy 2:15 that women are saved not by faith but by bearing children.

Principle 11 is valid. The case for keeping women subordinate in the church has rested on only three passages, ignoring dozens of passages on human unity in Christ, women leaders in the early church, giving of gifts by the Holy Spirit without regard for sex, and so forth.

Principle 12 is valid. The influence of the oral traditions on I Timothy 2 cannot be ignored. [**See special instructions for the exercise on Genesis 1 and 2.**]

Genesis 1 emphasizes that humanity is God's creative masterpiece by use of climactic order. Everything else is created first, with Adam and Eve as the climax of creation on the sixth day. Genesis 2 emphasizes that humanity is the climax of creation by use of the poetic "ring-effect," that is, by beginning and ending with the most important idea, Adam and Eve (the human race). But traditional interpreters used Genesis 2 (the idea of Adam first and then Eve) as a way of proving that women were *inferior* to men, something the text never says. The author of I Timothy 2 followed that tradition.

Principle 13 is valid. The Bible moves toward a vision of oneness and harmony in Christ, and neither I Timothy 2:11–15 nor any other passage should be used to refute or negate that central vision. When certain passages seem to contradict the central message of Scripture, we must suspect that the human authors have allowed some of their human biases to come to the fore. The Bible is a book that is both human and holy.

Special Instructions for Session Five

FOR THE EXERCISE CONCERNING PRINCIPLES OF INTERPRETATION. *GROUP:* You as leader should read the principles aloud slowly and clearly, sticking with one until everyone has had time to decide whether that principle is right or wrong. Group members should not copy the whole principle but should merely number from 1 to 13 and mark each principle (by number) as *Right* (valid) or *Wrong* (invalid).

Here are the principles. Read them over as often as necessary to make them clear to your group members.

Principle 1. A knowledge of the original languages—Greek, Aramaic, and Hebrew—is necessary for a full and completely accurate factual interpretation of the Bible.

Principle 2. It is vital to take into account the cultural background of the various books of the Bible.

Principle 3. Key words should be defined as they were defined at the time of the first writing and reading, including consideration of popular figures of speech at the time, because we are primarily concerned with understanding what the author originally intended.

Principle 4. When biblical references are obscure, such as the reference in I Corinthians 15:29 to being baptized for the dead, it is best to say we do not know.

Principle 5. A given passage of scripture ultimately has only one literal meaning (interpretation) but may have several moral implications (applications).

Principle 6. If a biblical passage touches on history or science, we should check our interpretation with secular studies in geology, biology, history, anthropology, classical literature, and so forth.

Principle 7. Our specific interpretations should frequently be checked against great doctrinal documents and scholarly doctrinal studies to be sure we have not departed from the major themes of the Bible, since such departures would violate the "rule of faith."

Principle 8. We must approach the Bible inductively, letting it speak for itself, trying hard to free ourselves from our personal prejudices, biases, and traditions.

Principle 9. When the grammar permits a choice between an obvious, clear, rational interpretation and an obscure, recondite interpretation that strains the reader's credulity, the interpreter should choose the clearer and more rational interpretation.

Principle 10. In the overall interpretation of any biblical doctrine, clear passages should govern our interpretation of more obscure passages.

Principle 11. Any teaching should be based not on one or two brief passing references to a topic but rather on *extensive* scriptural references.

Principle 12. Careful attention must be paid to the individual personalities of the authors of the various books of the Bible—to the literary forms they choose, to their unique use of words, to their personal preferences for certain figures of speech, to the influence of their education and experiences upon their way of expressing themselves, and so forth.

Principle 13. Christians interpret the Bible as one whole, harmonious system of doctrine centering around the person of Christ, so that no one passage may be interpreted out of the context of this central system. *INDIVIDUAL:* Number from 1 to 13 and mark each principle listed above as *Right* (valid) or *Wrong* (invalid).

FOR EXERCISE CONCERNING I TIMOTHY 2:11–15. *GROUP:* Have someone read the passage aloud while everyone else follows. Then ask the group to talk about the various questions that this passage raises in their minds. Go over each phrase, asking yourselves what it means and whether it seems to contradict other passages in the Bible. *INDIVIDUAL:* Make a list (mental or written) of all the problems you encounter in this passage. [SEE GROUP INSTRUCTIONS.]

FOR EXERCISES CONCERNING THE SITUATION AT EPHESUS. *GROUP:* Ask your group to make an imaginative reconstruction of what might have been going on in Timothy's congregation at Ephesus. Share with them the following hints: (1) In I Timothy 2:11–15, the phrase translated "woman [should] learn in silence" uses a word suggesting proper decorum, desisting from bustle. The same word is used in I

Timothy 2:2 which urges all Christians to live "a tranquil and quiet life" (NEB). (2) The word for *teach* means "formal teaching." (3) I Timothy 5:15 and II Timothy 3:6–7 indicate that Timothy's congregation had been involved in false doctrines. (4) In I Timothy 2:12, "to [have] authority over the man" means "to interrupt, to dictate to, to domineer over, to lord it over." (5) The word *men* probably refers to husbands. (6) Ephesus was the center for the worship of the goddess Diana. *INDIVIDUAL:* Follow group instructions, trying to get a vivid mental picture of the local situation in Ephesus.

FOR GALATIANS 3:28. *GROUP:* Explain to the group that every New Testament passage concerning women in the church occurs in a setting of local, specific, practical problems except for Galatians 3:28, the only passage that places the status of women in a *doctrinal* context. Read the passage aloud and then discuss how this passage ought to affect the passages about female silence which are placed in the context of specific local situations. *INDIVIDUAL:* Think through the issue raised in the group instructions.

FOR THE EXERCISE CONCERNING "AUTHENTEIN." *GROUP:* Explain that according to the way it is used in classical Greek drama, the word *authentein,* translated in I Timothy 2:12 as "to [have] authority over," is used in connection sometimes with suicide, sometimes with family murder, and sometimes with lordship or acting like an autocrat. Ask the group to discuss what those actions or attitudes have in common and what light they throw on I Timothy's comment concerning women's "authority" over men. *INDIVIDUAL:* Think through the issue raised in the group instructions.

FOR THE EXERCISE ON GENESIS 1 AND 2. *GROUP:* Ask each person to make two columns on a sheet of paper with headings of Genesis 1 and Genesis 2. In column 1, list each thing that was created, in the order it is given in Genesis 1. In column 2, list each thing that was created, in the order given in Genesis 2. Then discuss which order the I Timothy 2 passage follows. Examine the Genesis text to see if it lends any support to the conclusion drawn in I Timothy 2 that the order of creation gives males more authority to teach than females. *INDIVIDUAL:* Make your parallel-column lists and think through the issues raised in the group instructions.

Between Now and the Sixth (Final) Session

If you marked all thirteen of the principles of biblical interpretation *Right* (valid), give yourself an A+! More importantly, do your best to put all of them into practice in your own study of the Bible. And please read chapters 5 and 6 of *Women, Men, and the Bible*.

Session Six:
Bible Doctrines and Human Equality

HOW TO PREPARE FOR THIS SESSION

For this session you will need a Bible, a pencil or pen, paper, and your own meditative and imaginative faculties.

Summary of Major Ideas in Session Six (For use of group leaders only. Individuals should not read the summary until after doing all exercises.)

Many people have made a huge distinction between the concepts of love and justice. [**See special instructions for the exercise concerning definitions of love and justice.**]
Before discussing the definitions, we can test our own practical attitudes by sharing reactions to a single fact. [**See**

special instructions for exercise concerning church secretaries.]

Galatians 5:14 tells us to love our neighbor as ourself. If we regard exploited, underpaid church secretaries as our neighbors, we will be hurt by the injustice they endure and will be eager to do something to correct it. Biblically, definitions of justice would have to include righteousness, impartiality, and fairness. And love in the Bible involves unselfish loyalty and benevolent concern for the other. So there is an enormous overlap between love and justice. Ephesians 4:24 makes a *just* and devout life the sign of the new nature in Christ; elsewhere, that sign is called *love*.

Love often goes beyond justice; but we cannot fall beneath the standards of justice in our treatment of others and say that we love them.

Loving behavior must be built on a foundation of justice.

John Stott defined both love and submission as "the total giving of yourself to another." So when the wife submits and the husband loves, they are both doing the same thing— giving themselves to each other, going far beyond mere justice, yet certainly being just to each other as part of their love. "Love" that exploits is not love at all.

Biblical feminists ask that Christians treat one another with justice in fulfillment of the great law of love. As Romans 13:8– 10 says, "Love cannot wrong a neighbor" (v. 10*a* NEB) since "the whole law is summed up in love" (v. 10*b* NEB). Therefore, the Christian community should cease wronging women, should cease wronging *anybody*. [See special instructions for the exercise concerning justice for everybody.]

The concept of human equality is based not only on the pervasive New Testament doctrine of love but also on the doctrine of creation in the image of God, on the doctrine of the incarnation of Jesus the Christ in human flesh, and on biblical indications that each person of the Trinity is to be thought of not only as masculine but also as feminine.

Still another Bible doctrine that undergirds human equality is that of the immanence and transcendence of God. *Transcendence* means that God is greater than the sum of the creation—infinite, all-powerful, all-knowing. *Immanence* means that because God is infinite, God's power and intelligence and goodness embrace and penetrate all creation. So God is not only *above* us but *within* us (John 1:12; Proverbs 20:27; I John 4:16).

It is unthinkable that anyone can deliberately exploit or scorn or require subordination of any category of persons in whom the presence of God is recognized. [See special instructions for the exercise concerning Luke 1:26–55.]

Although some contemporary preachers advocate that every woman must relate to God through a male "umbrella of authority" or a male superior in the "chain of command," Mary did not consult Joseph about bearing Jesus but rather related to God's messenger very directly; and Genesis 2:22–23 records the fact that Eve had a direct personal relationship with God before she ever met Adam.

Luke 1:26–55 indicates that Mary was not submitting to an external force but rather to the will of God that existed within her as well as extended beyond her. The angel said the Sovereign was with her; she identified herself as the Sovereign's servant; and in the Magnificat she indicated that *God* also had served *her,* filling the hungry and ranging Godself at the side of God's servant Israel.

Like Mary, we achieve spiritual greatness only by aligning our wills with a will that goes beyond ourselves and into concern for the whole family of God.

None of us, male or female, seems fully enough aware of the fact that God is in us and we in God. [See special instructions concerning the meditation on Galatians 3:27.]

Not only our individual selves but also our family, friends, and acquaintances will achieve their ideal humanity by becoming one in Christ Jesus. [**See special instructions for the meditation on oneness in Christ.**]

Paradoxically, becoming one person in the Christ does not mean we lose our individuality; but we do learn to care about other human beings as we care for our own hands, feet, and eyes.

If we are all one person in the Christ, there can be no categorizing of persons as dominant and submissive, important and unimportant. Only God dictates the various functions within the body, by means of bestowing the gifts needed for the job the individual was created to do. [**See special instructions for the meditation on relative importance.**]

Just as it is important not to hurt or to wrong anyone else in the Body of Christ, it is just as important not to hurt or wrong ourselves. All of us become equally important because we are in God and God is in us.

We live either in fear or in love; perfect love banishes fear (I John 4:18). Since relationships between men and women have been characterized by deep fear for a very long time, we need to learn how to be more truly loving. [**See special instructions concerning meditation on oneness with an "enemy".**]

Seeing an "enemy" clothed in Christ does not mean, of course, that we must wrong ourselves by submitting to endless abuse from that person. But we can learn to speak only to that person's ideal humanity, to what that person would be like if he or she were fully loving and living in the spirit of Christ. Even should withdrawal be necessary in order to avoid further abuse, we can still love the "enemy" through prayer.

The biblical light on male-female relationships, and on all relationships, is well summarized in Ephesians 4:22 and following. We must leave the old ways of female inferiority and subordination and be made new in mind and spirit, recognizing our *oneness* as the members of Christ's one body. And we must practice mutual submission out of reverence for Christ.

Special Instructions for Session Six

FOR THE EXERCISE CONCERNING DEFINITIONS OF LOVE AND JUSTICE. *GROUP:* Ask group members to write down what they consider to be an adequate definition of justice and an adequate definition of love, using no more than one sentence for each. Then share the definitions with one another. Try, as a group, to recall any Bible passages that help to define the relationship between love and the law (or justice), and discuss their implications. *INDIVIDUAL:* Write down your definitions of love and justice and, if you like, check them against the definitions in a standard dictionary. Try to recall Bible passages on the relationship between love and law (justice).

FOR THE EXERCISE CONCERNING CHURCH SEC-RETARIES. *GROUP:* Try to get each person involved in expressing personal *feelings* concerning this one fact: Within the past several years, over 50 percent of the church secretaries in the United States were paid less than $2.40 an hour for their highly skilled labor (that amounts to less than $5,000 a year for full-time work). *INDIVIDUAL:* Think out your attitude toward the fact outlined above in the group exercise.

FOR THE EXERCISE CONCERNING JUSTICE FOR EVERYBODY. *GROUP:* Ask everybody to jot down a list of practical changes that would come about in churches and homes if everybody took seriously the law of justice in love. Then share your lists with one another. See if you can get your group to become more openly personal. For instance, would anyone be willing to share one specific change he or she plans to make in personal behavior in obedience to the law of justice in love? *INDIVIDUAL:* Make your own list according to the group instructions, and think about how you can contribute to bringing about such changes.

FOR THE EXERCISE CONCERNING LUKE 1:26–55.

GROUP: After reading the passage aloud, ask group members to find *in the passage* the answers to two questions: (1) Did Mary relate to God through a human male intermediary? (2) Was Mary asked to subordinate her will to a will that was completely external to herself? *INDIVIDUAL:* Think through the above issues; then read the summary under this topic.

FOR THE MEDITATION ON GALATIANS 3:27. *GROUP:* After reading aloud Galatians 3:27 in as many translations as the group possesses, ask everybody to close their eyes and to sit silently, making a mental image of the Christ clothed in shining light. Then picture the Christ's coming toward you and dressing you in a shining personality. Be wrapped in this light. Watch your personality become Christlike, or ideally human. Concentrate on "Christ in you, the hope of glory," and on *putting on the Christ "as a garment." INDIVIDUAL:* Follow group instructions.

FOR THE MEDITATION ON ONENESS IN THE CHRIST. *GROUP:* This time, close your eyes and imagine not just yourself but all your family and acquaintances being dressed in the Christ's shining light. Try to include both males and females and members of races and economic levels different from your own. Include some unbelievers, envisioning them as you would like them to be, in Christ. Watch everybody, yourself included, being covered by the shining glory of the Christ. *INDIVIDUAL:* Follow group instructions.

FOR THE MEDITATION ON RELATIVE IMPORTANCE. *GROUP:* With eyes closed, reconstruct your last picture of yourself and your acquaintances and family wrapped in the garment of the Christ, the New Humanity. Examine that picture to see who is more important. Are some persons more important than others? Why? After giving yourself plenty of time to enter into this vision, share the results with one another. *INDIVIDUAL:* Follow group instructions, perhaps jotting down your reactions as to which persons are more important than others, if indeed any are. Then check the summary on this topic.

FOR MEDITATION ON ONENESS WITH AN "EN-EMY." *GROUP:* Close your eyes and picture clearly one person, preferably of the other sex, who makes you feel irritated and put down or angry and threatened. See yourself standing next to that person. Then picture the Christ's coming toward both of you, embracing you both in a robe of shining light. Let the other person's nastiness—and your own fear—disappear into Christ's nature. Let your personalities be clothed in the Christ; picture the other person and yourself manifesting Christlike love toward each other. Keep at it until you get a good look at the personality transformation. *INDI-VIDUAL:* Follow group instructions.

Assignment for the Future

Please read chapter 7 of *Women, Men, and the Bible.* Although this is the last session in this series, I hope the concepts will become a living part of you because of your dedication to justice and human equality through loving mutual submission.